BLACK MASCULINITY IN THE OBAMA ERA

Black Masculinity in the Obama Era

Outliers of Society

William T. Hoston

palgrave
macmillan

BLACK MASCULINITY IN THE OBAMA ERA
Copyright © William T. Hoston, 2014.

First published in 2014 by
PALGRAVE MACMILLAN®
in the United States—a division of St. Martin's Press LLC,
175 Fifth Avenue, New York, NY 10010.

Where this book is distributed in the UK, Europe and the rest of the world,
this is by Palgrave Macmillan, a division of Macmillan Publishers Limited,
registered in England, company number 785998, of Houndmills,
Basingstoke, Hampshire RG21 6XS.

Palgrave Macmillan is the global academic imprint of the above companies
and has companies and representatives throughout the world.

Palgrave® and Macmillan® are registered trademarks in the United States,
the United Kingdom, Europe and other countries.

ISBN: 978–1–137–43619–1

Library of Congress Cataloging-in-Publication Data

Hoston, William T.
    Black masculinity in the Obama era : outliers of society / by William
T. Hoston.
       pages cm
    Includes bibliographical references and index.
    ISBN 978–1–137–43619–1 (hardcover : alk. paper)
       1. Masculinity—United States—History—21st century. 2. African
American men—History—21st century. 3. Obama, Barack. I. Title.

BF692.5.H67 2014
155.8'49607300811—dc23   2014006207

A catalogue record of the book is available from the British Library.

Design by Newgen Knowledge Works (P) Ltd., Chennai, India.

First edition: August 2014

10 9 8 7 6 5 4 3 2 1

To
My Godfather
Andrew "Sonny" Owens
The only father I have ever known…
I've been knocking on God's door since birth/ My biological
father didn't want me/
I prayed to the Holy Father and he gave me a Godfather/
To witness my testimony/
Thank you

CONTENTS

ILLUSTRATIONS

FIGURE

TABLES

ACKNOWLEDGMENTS

All praise to my Lord and savior, Jesus Christ. With Him, all things are possible. He has provided me with the four most influential women in my life, the late Mildred Hoston, the late Bertha-Mae Mitchell, Thelma C. Owens, and Janet Smith.

Thank you to the many people who contributed to making this book possible. First, I would like to thank my research assistant, Imee L. Smith, for countless hours of research. To my mentor, Dr. Ronald Dorris, your input was invaluable to this project. To one of my favorite students, Tiffani Cullum, thank you for the many proofreading sessions and suggestions. Finally, I am grateful to the folks at Palgrave MacMillan for believing in this project. Thanks to Lani Oshima, Mara Berkoff, and Rachel Taenzler for assisting me through the final stages of completion.

To my darling mother, Janet Smith; her examples of faith, courage, and sacrifice gave me much inspiration over the years to follow my dreams.

Thank you to all the Black males who participated in this project. I am forever grateful for your contributions. To my nephew, J-Gutta, my rock, I love you.

To you whom I have not named, please know that even though you are not named in this book, I deeply appreciate what you have contributed to my life. Your contributions have helped this "Black boy fly."

Introduction

Some years ago, while a graduate teaching assistant instructing a *Social Problems of Youth* course at Florida State University (FSU), I assigned the class an extra credit assignment to watch the HBO documentary *Thug Life in D.C.* The documentary explores the lives of young Black males locked behind bars in Washington, DC. Filmmakers Marc Levin and Daphne Pinkerson present a raw and uncut reality of the generation of young Black males who have been criminalized. Many of these individuals came from poverty-stricken ghettos, single-parent households, and were devoid of a proper education. While the documentary focuses mainly on Aundrey Burno, a 17-year-old convicted felon facing 115 years in prison for the attempted murder of a police officer, the correctional officer in the documentary was the person (for me) who most stood out.

The correctional officer's brash, straightforward approach is startling, yet needed when interacting with particular young Black males, especially those who have been criminalized and have become victims of generational psychological slavery. At one point in the documentary, the officer explains how he is able to endure the day-to-day grind of working in the harsh environment of a correctional facility:

> You know how I am able to survive in here everyday? Because I tell these young men the truth. I give them an education you don't give them from one to 16-years-old in your D.C. public schools. I tell them what it is like to be a *real nigga* in America. What is expected of them. What they must go through. How they must program. And how to stay alive and *avoid* this system [emphasis added].

When discussing the extra credit assignment in class, one of my students expressed that he liked the aggressive, no-nonsense, disposition of the correctional officer and his advice to the young Black men. However, he suggested that maybe if those in correctional facilities would have heard this advice prior to being locked up, this may have helped to deter criminal actions that led to them being incarcerated—similar to the *Scared Straight* program. Another student countered that opinion and suggested that these young Black males would be better served not by yelling and trying to intimidate them, but by having a conversation with them. However, that conversation must involve older, successful Black males whose backgrounds transcend those of their younger counterparts. They need to hear not only from former drug dealers, hustlers, and pimps, to whom many were exposed prior to being incarcerated, but also from current doctors, professors, and lawyers.

The correctional officer went on to assess the state of young Black males in this country. He stated:

> I see him. I hear him. I listen to his music. He has no hope. He has no reason to go on. And one day, his generation is going to lose it. You better understand why they [are] so emotional. Why they shoot so much. Why they don't care about life. Because nobody is giving them any reason to care.

His assessment, along with the class discussion, weighed heavily on me. These students, like so many other scholars who have attempted to study the pathology of Black males, wanted answers. They wanted answers to the root cause of Black male behavior that eventually leads them to one of two avenues—convicted felons branded by the criminal justice system or death.

Later that day, I attended my graduate statistics course whereby the professor talked about statistical outlier detection. An *outlier* is defined as an observation on a statistical graph that visually appears to be distant from other observations in the data output (see figure 0.1). Simply, the outlier

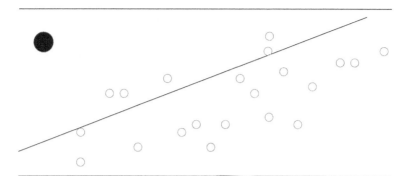

Figure 0.1 Example of a Statistical Outlier.

appears as though it has been excluded from the rest of the observations on the statistical graph—a Black dot.

The professor made a compelling argument during the lecture that it is important to study outliers, which often contain vital information about the data output. Before considering the possible elimination or discrediting the importance of the outlier, we should try to understand their existence and whether it is likely that similar outliers will continue to appear. To properly handle an outliner, a process should begin immediately to determine its root cause.

This lecture moved me to think. How does this apply to Black males? According to the 2010 US Census, Blacks were 13.6 percent of the US population. Five percent of US citizens were Black males. Historically, racial discrimination and disparities have highlighted the struggles of Black males. They continue to be policed at an alarming percentage, disproportionately incarcerated, disenfranchised by partial voting rights, and face institutional and systemic barriers that at times deny equal access to employment, job promotion, and formal education. Throughout history, the social construct of America has attempted to discredit their importance and plight without trying to understand the devastating effects of slavery and continued discrimination. Black males can be considered *outliers*.

Since 1619, when the first African slaves came to America, Black people, especially Black males, have been outliers. The 300-year captivity of Africans is not merely an event of the past; it still has relevance. Black male slaves were treated differently than their female counterparts. Slave owners were afraid of their physical appearance and strength. They forbid these slaves from assuming the traditional roles of male dominance and control. Male slaves performed hard labor and were subjected to harsh punishment. In comparison, Black female slaves endured similar hardships, however the methods of abuse were different. Female slaves were highly subjected to sexual abuse. Their advantages were that some became the sexual mistress of the slave owners, developed interdependent relationships with the wives of slave owners and the children they cared for on the plantation, which helped them cope with the inhumane treatment. Black male slaves, as a rule, did not develop interdependent relationships that established emotional bonds. In most cases, they did not even establish bonds with female slaves who could be subjected to sexual abuse from the slave owner. Many believed they were in jeopardy of being sold, which made them less likely to establish certain bonds.

The mental control of slave owners over Black male slaves hindered their ability to have a formable identity on the plantation. The physical, mental, and verbal abuse toward Black male slaves made them an outlier since arriving in the United States. Conceivably written in 1712, the *Willie Lynch Writings: Let's Make a Slave* articulates that the mission of the slave owner was to break Black male slaves from their natural state of masculinity. This was done to sustain mental and physical control over Black male slaves, ultimately reducing them to a mere shell of themselves. The document informs, "I have a [*sic*] full proof method for controlling your Black slaves. I guarantee everyone of you that if installed correctly it will control the slaves for at least 300 years" (Hassan-El 1999, 2). Relative to the time the document was written, the mental and physical grasp should have expired in 2012. But with more Black males now facing jail than enslaved in 1850, the lasting effects of Willie Lynch's methods seem to be alive and well. As Michelle Alexander so clearly shows in her highly acclaimed book, *The New Jim Crow: Mass Incarceration in the Age of Colorblindness* (2010), tough approaches to crime mirror that of slavery and are used as a form of social control on Black males.

When social scientists are attempting to research the root cause of the inexplicable behavior of a sample of Black males, history declares that slavery has been a good starting point. However, what in the twenty-first century continues to be the root cause of their behavior? Why is there continual discrimination and racism against Black males? Are Black males still victims of discrimination and racism? Or, are these actions toward them and pointed racial stereotypes now self-inflicted? Have Black males become their own worst enemies?

Of course, many Black males never get arrested, and do not go to prison. They fulfill civic duties, graduate from high school and college, obtain well-paying jobs, and go on to live successful lives. There are examples of Black males who have made significant achievements. Some grew up in the inner-city surrounded by poverty, gangs, and violence, but those negative forces were never pervasive enough to deter them from being successful. Hence, we cannot ignore the disparity between those who have overcome their individual circum stances and institutional barriers versus those who have not.

The continual plight of the Black male deserves attention far beyond the statistical grid, which often does not provide an accurate narrative. One important diagnosis is that statistical outliers can be caused by errors in measurement. Has history led us to an erroneous perception of Black males? How do we measure the plight of Black males? We are concerned about outliers on a statistical graph given the possible effect on the estimates of a (White America) and b (Black America) and as a result affect the fit (or their fit between and/or within the two Americas). This is similar to what W.

E. B. DuBois (1903) in *The Souls of Black Folk* describes as a "warring soul." It is the warring ideal of having to subsist between White America and Black America in one dark body. How does the Black male assimilate? Is he willing to assimilate? And, if he is unwilling to assimilate, does he then become an outlier? *Is the Black male simply a "black dot" in a socially constructed White world, and unwilling to conform and integrate, never gaining the ability to be indistinguishable from other members in American society?*

The Florida State University statistics class has stuck with me for years. I vowed that when I got to a specific time and place in my academic career, my intent would be to write a book that encapsulates the Black male experience. In 2008, when Barack Hussein Obama was elected as the 44th president of the United States and the first Black president, I initially thought a book that contains this type of dialogue no longer is needed. However, to the contrary, it was needed more than ever. While the 2008 presidential election was the most defining moment for Black Americans in the twenty-first century, many Black males were distressed by Obama's election and others did not believe he was "Black enough" to hold such a position in Black history. He also had to disassociate himself from his longtime religious mentor and personal advisor, Rev. Jeremiah A. Wright Jr., after Wright made controversial remarks that threatened Obama's candidacy. PBS talk show host Tavis Smiley and scholar Cornel West went on a "poverty tour" to chastise the president for his lack of concern for the economic state of the Black community. The differing opinions among Black males about Obama and whether he has helped to reduce the negative perceptions of them or provokes racial resentment is central to writing this book.

In *Black Masculinity in the Obama Era* I venture forth to expand the discussion on the economic, social, and political plight of Black males in the twenty-first century. The purpose of this book is to provide an in-depth examination of the current state of Black males, and to identify the impact of living in the Obama era. To begin the process of writing this book, I asked over 100 Black males one primary open-ended question, "What does it mean to be a Black male in the twenty-first century?" This was done with the intent to encourage meaningful dialogue using their own experiences to springboard themes throughout the book. I also did this in an effort to build on previous findings of social scientists that historically have provided suggestive and mixed results about the pathology of Black males. A myriad of quantitative over qualitative research has been conducted to examine the life experiences of Black males from underprivileged backgrounds. Many of those studies have lacked an in-depth understanding of Black male behavior and are void of effective remedies to deal with their problems. As scholar Orlando Patterson explains in his 2006 opinion editorial, *A Poverty of the Mind*:

> The main cause for this shortcoming is a deep-seated dogma that has prevailed in social science and policy circles since the mid-1960's: the rejection of any explanation that invokes a group's cultural attributes—its distinctive attitudes, values and predispositions, and the resulting behavior of its members—and the relentless preference for relying on structural factors like low incomes, joblessness, poor schools and bad housing.[1]

Some researchers have been reluctant to engage in intense personal dialogue when they venture into the environment of Black males to hear about experiences told from their perspective to amass a more refined exchange to their research questions.

To understand the behavior of Black males in the twenty-first century, we must attempt to dissect the multiple layers tied to the life course of their own individual experiences. What better time to continue this exploration than in the age of the first Black president? What has been the impact of the "Obama Effect?" Has his presidency and presence had a profound effect on the Black community, particularly Black males?

After asking the participants, "what does it mean to be a Black male in the twenty-first century?" and several follow-up questions adopted from the social science discipline, a number of concerns emerged: (1) Black males felt that they were still thought of as "invisible" in White America; (2) the cultural identity of the Black male is often stripped to achieve the American Dream; (3) there is a generational shift in Black male identity; (4) misogynist and violence rap lyrics continue to have a negative influence on the Black male culture and create divisiveness among Black males and females; (5) Black-on-Black murders remain an epidemic in the inner-city; (6) the negative perceptions of Black males as criminals, low-skilled, and uneducated continue to plague their plight; and (7) the "Obama Effect" has not had the expected positive influence as initially intended to promote Black male achievement.

The above concerns are key in the organization of the chapters culminating into this book. Chapter One looks at the cultural identity of the Black male. This chapter focuses on the generational shift in Black male identity and on whether the younger generation of Black males has redefined the current Black male identity. Chapter Two explores the influence of misogynist rap lyrics, specifically those that promote the sexual assault and rape of Black women. The objective of this chapter is to open a dialogue about whether lyrics that celebrate the objectification and sexual abuse of women influence the thinking and behavior of Black males.

Chapter Three is a case study of Black-on Black murders in Chicago. For over a decade the city has had one of the highest murder totals of Black males in the United States. The troubling numbers have brought national attention and sparked intense dialogue among the participants in the book. It is fitting to provide a case study that examines this epidemic and the determinants of these murders. Chapter Four discusses the influence that President Obama has had on Black males. This chapter investigates the impact of the "Obama Effect" and whether the election and presence of a Black president has helped to reduce the negative perceptions of Black males and has led to increased Black male achievement. In Chapter Five, an effective set of individual strategies is offered for Black males to practice addressing the negative structural and cultural factors they face to help alleviate their current condition.

This book is a contribution to American discourse shaped by the perspectives of Black males. It gives readers the opportunity to look at the world through their eyes. They offer a rich and engaging discussion on issues relevant to the Black male subculture. The content in this book is raw, uncut, eye-opening, and takes a no-holds-barred approach to gain the attention of a wider audience and greater majority of Black males that could benefit from reading this study—even those who have made the unflattering statement, "I don't like to read" or "I hate to read." The language at intervals is strong and uncensored and speaks directly to this generation of Black males and an older generation. In order to have a critical dialogue with Black males in the twenty-first century, their thoughts have to be recorded as stated in interviews, songs, movies, and other outlets that portray Black male life and not refined to fit in the box of academic and societal acceptance. From critical discourse, dialogue, discussion, and conversation to barbershop talk, shooting the shit, or as this young Black male generation calls it, "choppin' it up," a hardline exchange of intellectual thought and action from social scientists, policy makers, activists, and concerned folks alike is needed to improve the current state of this generation of Black males.

CHAPTER 1

The Black Male Identity

If there is anyone out there who still doubts that America is a place where all things are possible; who still wonders if the dream of our founders is alive in our time; who still questions the power of our democracy, tonight is your answer.

—*President-Elect Barack H. Obama, November 4, 2008, Chicago, Illinois*

On November 4, 2008, Black Americans, as well as many Democrats, shed tears of joy while witnessing the election of Senator Barack H. Obama of Illinois as the country's first Black president. He was elected the forty-fourth president of the United States with 53 percent of the popular vote and 365 Electoral College votes, far exceeding the 270 threshold to capture the presidential office. The election of Obama was a significant moment in Black American history. This was a moment to be cherished for members of the Black community and African ancestry who had struggled for centuries to obtain economic, social, and political equality.

Since the election of President Obama, what are the continuing economic, social, and political challenges faced by the Black community, particularly Black males? Has the election of Obama changed the discourse among Black males? Has the societal perception of his achievement been a catalyst to alter negative stereotypes that haunt the Black male image? Has Obama's presence sparked added motivation for more Black males to strive to alleviate themselves from circumstances that may burden their progress or advancement?

Much discussion has taken place about the "Obama Effect" on Black males. His attainment of the highest executive position in the United States should serve as a model to inspire Black males to reach their full potential void of excuses perpetuated by institutional and systemic discrimination and racism. However, limited retort has directly surveyed the opinions of Black males regarding the impact of the "Obama Effect" and what issues continue to be of grave importance to Black males during his presidency.

Many social observers, Black and White, believe that since Obama has been elected to the presidential office, Black males no longer face the same discriminatory barriers as before. Their perception is that we have moved beyond institutional and systemic discrimination that has in the past crippled the plight of Black males. Needless to say, Obama's presence alone cannot cure the social ills that impact Black males. The symbolic achievement of one man cannot erase the centuries of injustices against masses of Black males.

The ideal of Obama as a symbol of Black male progress is rather ironic considering that during his 2008 presidential run many Blacks did not consider him a Black American and questioned the validity of his "Blackness." This part of his cultural identity was initially debated in the Black community. Cultural identity refers to "the attribution of a set of qualities to a given population" identified by a number of demographics such as race, ethnicity, gender, and social class (Friedman 1994, 29). Obama's race was at the center of the national spotlight and the validity of his "Blackness" was thought to be a deciding factor of whether he would be able to attract potential Black voters and appeal to the Black community as a legitimate candidate. His biracial heritage that includes an African father from Kenya and a White mother from Kansas made many in the Black community skeptical of his allegiance and commitment to representing Black interests.

In Obama's 1995 book, *Dreams from My Father*, he explains the influence of his Caucasian roots and discusses how his mother mostly shaped his cultural identity while his father was absent from his life. In a phase of Obama's life where his cultural identity takes shape and he begins to accept his identity as a Black American, he reflects:

> I knew it was too late to ever claim Africa as my home. And if I had come to understand myself as a black American, and was understood as such, that understanding remained unanchored to place. What I needed was a community, I realized, a community that cut deeper than the common despair that black friends and I shared when reading the latest crime statistics, or the high fives I might exchange on a basketball court. A place where I could put down stakes and test my commitments. (115)

Obama's understanding of community and awareness of the needs of the Black community propelled him to be an agent of social and political change and become a community organizer on Chicago's South side. As a community organizer in the Altgeld Gardens public housing project in the mid-1980s, he was a tireless worker for this majority Black housing development where residents struggled financially, lived in dilapidated units, and faced the constant fear of crime.

The controversy surrounding Obama's "Blackness" caused extensive debate in mainstream media. In October of 2006 when *Time Magazine* contributor Joe Klein wrote an article on Obama suggesting he could be "The Next President," members of the Black media offered a barrage of critical and harsh comments. Stanley Crouch, a Black columnist for the *New York Daily News*, wrote some pointed words in a November 2006 editorial titled "What Obama isn't: Black like me on race." He expresses, "Obama's mother is of white U.S. stock. His father is a black Kenyan. Other than color, Obama did not—does not—share a heritage with the majority of black Americans, who are descendants of plantation slaves."[1] These comments drew strong criticism from Obama supporters. Crouch further states:

> If he [Obama] throws his hat in the ring, he will have to run as the son of a white woman and an African immigrant. If we then

end up with him as our first black President, he will have come into the White House through a side door—which might, at this point, be the only one that's open.[2]

Crouch's comments were followed by Black writer Debra Dickerson on the liberal online website, *Salon*. In her 2007 editorial titled "Colorblind," Dickerson advised against "lumping us all together" for the benefit of recognizing Obama as a "Black man." Her claim was that "Black, in our political and social vocabulary, means those descended from West African slaves."[3] However, such criticism of defining "Blackness" is debatable, as cultural identity is not simply relegated to skin color but includes a number of demographic identifiers that shapes one's identity.

In *Dreams from My Father*, Obama recognizes that many would question his biracial identity. He recalls, "My father looked nothing like the people around me—that he was black as pitch, my mother white as milk—barely registered in my mind" (10). As a rule to the ideology of the one-drop theory that in the past assumed that a single drop of "Black blood" classified someone as Black, Obama is considered by many to be a Black American. In a 2008 CNN interview with Charlie Rose while on the campaign trail, Obama addressed the "Blackness" debate by stating, "If I'm outside your building trying to catch a cab they're not saying, 'Oh, there's a mixed race guy.'"[4]

The heightened condemnation of Obama's presidential run and need for proof of his "Blackness" spawned from the lack of cultural similarities with those in the Black community. Academic and friend of the Obama family, the late Ronald Walters, in a 2007 article that discussed Obama's Blackness, writes:

> It is legitimate that Black Americans raise questions about "Blackness" as an objective issue, because it is the core concept that defines the basic cultural identity of Black people. That is why the cultural identity of Barack Obama evoked such confusion. (12–13)

In his analysis, Walters indicates that Obama possessed a different cultural background than most Black Americans by living in different geographical areas thus making it difficult to relate to his life's journey. He expresses that, "his [Obama] identity omitted many of the cultural markers with which Blacks are more familiar to the extent that it has promoted a curiosity of 'cultural fit' that in turn has become an issue of political trust" (13).

Despite questioning Obama's "Blackness" because he had an African father, White mother, was raised by White grandparents, grew up in Hawaii, and had a brief stint in Indonesia, he did have a number of specific cultural markers many in the Black community could relate to that molded his cultural identity and should have provided acceptance in the Black community prior to his presidential run. First, he grew up without a father. Second, he is married to a Black woman, Michelle Obama. Third, he attended a majority Black church, Trinity United Church of Christ (TUCC), headed by Jeremiah A Wright Jr., for over twenty years before he denounced his affiliation amid public scrutiny. Last, he became a community organizer in Chicago and later a state legislator representing a majority Black district.

Cultural similarities are important markers in distinguishing Obama as a member of the Black community. For instance, on several occasions Obama has strongly advocated during his presidency for the presence of Black males in the home. He has expressed that the evolving cultural identity of the Black male is highly dependent on current Black fathers assuming parental responsibility and rearing a child to have a solid foundation for success. The absence of such a relationship has an adverse effect on the Black male identity. In *Dreams from My Father*, he recollects:

> At the time of his death, my father remained a myth to me, both more and less than a man. He had left Hawaii back in 1963, when I was only two years old, so that as a child I knew him only through the stories that my mother and grandparents

told. They all had their favorites, each one seamless, burnished smooth from repeated use. (5)

After a stretch of narrating positive, memorable stories told from the perspectives of his mother and grandfather, Obama enters a reflective mode and expresses, "My father was missing. He had left paradise, and nothing that my mother or grandparents told me could obviate that single, unassailable fact. Their stories didn't tell me why he had left" (26).

Obama, like so many other Black males, wanted to know why his father did not return. This question has lingered in the minds of many Black males who seek the answer for their own personal refuge. In a 2008 Father's Day address at the Apostolic Church of God on Chicago's South Side, Obama spoke to the congregation about his own experience growing up without a father and the responsibility needed on the part of Black males. In the speech, he voiced parental responsibility:

> But if we are honest with ourselves, we'll admit that what too many fathers also are is missing—missing from too many lives and too many homes. They have abandoned their responsibilities, acting like boys instead of men. And the foundations of our families are weaker because of it.
>
> We need fathers to realize that responsibility does not end at conception. We need them to realize that what makes you a man is not the ability to have a child—it's the courage to raise one.[5]

How can a man who grew up without his father, raised in a White culture, by his own admission experienced little racial discrimination, and was sheltered from life as a Black American in his childhood and adolescent years as told in the book *The Audacity of Hope* (2006) have a profound impact on other Black males? The answer is simple. Obama can have an impact the same way that a young Rev. Dr. Martin Luther King Jr. led a nation against racial injustice, discrimination, and admittedly said he was isolated from those same burdens as a youth.

The culmination of Obama's personal journey has been inspirational for the Black community. With a highly intelligent, regal, Black wife by his side, First Lady Michelle Obama, and two beautiful daughters, the Obamas represent a strong nuclear Black family. In particular, he represents the idea of what it means to be a God-fearing, strong, wholesome, loving, caring, highly educated family man that is in high demand in the Black community, in contrast to the constant negative societal portrayals of Black males as individuals who do not marry the mother of their children, have multiple children out of wedlock, are unemployed, uneducated, and considered criminal misfits.

Obama represents the twenty-first century's version of the "New Negro," a term promoted by Alain Locke in the 1920s during the Harlem Renaissance period that represented social and cultural change for Black Americans and catapulted positive and progressive images of Black males. Locke (1925) wrote in the foreword of the seminal text, *The New Negro: An Interpretation*, "Negro life is not only establishing new contacts and founding new centers, it is finding a new soul. There is a fresh spiritual and cultural focusing" (ix).

During the Obama era, similar to the times of the Harlem Renaissance and Civil Rights movement, the cultural identity of Black male life is at the center of this discussion. Cultural identity plays a significant role in the representation of one's self, both positively and negatively. It is difficult to dissect the multiple layers of the Black male identity, especially in one such as Obama. According to Gerald, Entrepreneur, 36:

> Obama is cool as hell. His identity is so complex, yet simple and refreshing.
>
> On one hand, he was the first Black president of the Harvard Law Review and later went on to become the first Black president of the United States. On the other hand, you see pictures of him with his wife and kids, chilling at the basketball game like an every day dude. He is such an inspiration. I love my president.

President Obama campaigned on "hope," "change," and "forward." We assume his presidential message of creating a better America had a profound effect on the 93 percent of Black voters who re-elected him in 2012. This strong commitment to Obama has led social scientists and political pundits to attempt to identify what has Obama's effect been on Black America? Proponents believe that Obama's transformational potential is unlimited and should have an awe-inspiring influence on the Black community as a whole, particularly Black males. On the contrary, some opponents have indicated that the "Obama Effect" may be waning, especially among Black males, and some were never swayed by his election and presence. For example, as I shall discuss in Chapter Four, criticism has loomed that Obama's presence may not have a significant influence on the lives of Black males and what the future holds for them.

Have the 2008 and 2012 elections of Obama created a new cultural narrative for Black males? What is the root cause of the continual discrimination and racism against Black males and the behavioral responses of this marginalized group? Are Black males still victims of discrimination and racism? Or, are these actions toward them and pointed racial stereotypes now self-inflicted? Have they become their own worst enemies? Can a majority of Black males assimilate and achieve the highest levels of economic, social, and political success? What has truly been the influence of President Obama on the plight of Black males? More importantly, what does it mean to be a Black male in the twenty-first century?

This book explores the current autonomous Black male subculture. The aim is to expand the discussion on the economic, social, and political plight of Black males in the twenty-first century. The fracture of Black solidarity since the Civil Rights movement, coupled with decades of limited productive opportunities and quality resources, leads this dialogue to first dissect the multiple layers of the Black male identity. What is the current cultural identity of Black males? And what role do structural factors such as job-lessness, poverty, and the broken-down public education system play in shaping their identity? As stated above, the identity of Black males is further magnified since the election of President Obama and the false notion that Black males now live in a "post-racial" America wherein "excuses" are no longer tolerated. On the one hand, Black males have made substantive progress. But in stark contradiction, the stratification of those who have achieved success and those who have not is a widening gap that deserves continual discourse.

Formation of the Black Male Identity

The American institution of slavery stripped the Black male of his identity. Long before the period of slavery, they were very influential and prominent male figures. Black males such as Imhotep, an African Egyptian, gifted in multiple disciplines such as architecture and medicine, had a profound impact on history. Imhotep was considered the "Father of Medicine" more than 2000 years before the West considered Hippocrates as the Father of Medicine. Imhotep was also recognized as the world's first architect, building Egypt's first pyramid in the year 2780 BC (Asante 2000). Throughout history there is evidence to prove that Greece was not the origin of civilization. Ancient Egypt was the base of African men who were intellectuals, architects, physicians, scientists, and theologians.

History books have provided a revisionist version of the early contributions of Black males. Many of the younger generation of Black males in the twenty-first century are unfamiliar with the history and legacy of their ancestors because, unfortunately, our school systems do not teach this lineage nor acknowledge the early contributions of African

Egyptians. Rap group Dead Prez explicitly points this out in the introduction of their 2000 song, "'They' Schools," claiming that the educational system does not favor the plight of Black Americans:

> Man that school shit is a joke/ The same people who control the school system control the prison system, and the whole social system/

The artists later go on to say in the song:

> I tried to pay attention but they classes wasn't interestin'/ They seemed to only glorify the Europeans/ Claimin' Africans were only three fifth's a human being/

Dead Prez's overall view of the public school system is that it does not educate Black students to be critical thinkers and teach them how to generate their own means of residual wealth, but rather "[schools] teach us nothing but how to be slaves and hardworkers for white people."

For many the history of Black Americans in the school system is often taught in a vacuum. To begin with, most educators do not accurately explain that *race* is not real. Race is a socially constructed concept to create divisions as a method of oppression. As Haney-Lopez (1994, 7) explains, "Race is neither an essence nor an illusion, but rather an ongoing, contradictory, self-reinforcing process subject to the macro forces of social and political struggle and the micro effects of daily decisions." Teaching the dichotomy of skin color, Black and White, at an early age negatively primes adolescents to feel they belong to a certain social group before fully understanding they are human beings. In many cases the concept of race is used to define their daily lives. But rather than teaching young Black males they are no different from their White counterparts, educators tend to start at some given point during slavery that highlights their differences. They quickly transition to 1863 when President Abraham Lincoln issued an Executive Order known as the Emancipation Proclamation that led to the freeing of the slaves only in those states in rebellion against the Union. Ending slavery in its entirety called for ratification of the 13th amendment in 1865. Afterward, segregation in the Jim Crow South was implemented for nearly another 100 years until key court decisions and legislation such as *Brown v. Board of Education* (1954), the Civil Rights Act of 1964, and Voting Rights Act of 1965 were enacted to set a precedent to gain equality.

In primary and secondary assigned history books, little attention is ever garnered to the plight of Black males after slavery. The masses of history books, most written by White scholars over time, provide a brief narrative of their triumphs and victories, which speaks directly to the development of their identity. These books make little mention of how Blacks fought in the Civil War (1861–1865) to help the North win, which was a huge step toward equal rights, or how Black males in the post–Civil War Reconstruction era openly served in the military as high-ranking officials and were able to vote and function as free men. Also, there is a dearth of teaching about the "Negro Movement" of the Harlem Renaissance in the 1920s, essential in identifying early key Black male figures in American history.

Black male pioneers who paved the way for continual Black achievement were Benjamin Banneker, Nat Turner, Frederick Douglass, Dr. Daniel Hale Williams, George Washington Carver, Marcus Garvey, W. E. B. DuBois, Booker T. Washington, James W. Johnson, Langston Hughes, Josh Gibson, Jesse Owens, Paul Robeson, Thurgood Marshall, and many more. Black male achievement has transcended into the 1950s, '60s, '70s, '80s, '90s, and the 2000s, culminating in the election of President Obama.

Most history courses in the school system would have Black males to believe three things about Black history—that slavery happened and White America is apologetic, a great White American president freed Black slaves, and the Civil Rights Movement was led by the Rev. Dr. Martin Luther King Jr., the most significant and nonradical Black leader to ever live. These discussions are void of the fact that Black males have contributed greatly to the fabric of American culture, ranging from political figures, educators, and inventors to entertainers and great athletes.

Early teachings in the school system play a central role in the formation of Black male identities and in shaping their psyches. When knowledge of self-worth starts at slavery, it can have an adverse effect leading to Black males struggling from childhood to adulthood in defining their identity. While the goal is to educate, an undesirable effect takes place in the teaching of inferiority. Educators explain to Black students that the institution of slavery tore them from their homes and forcibly transported them to Jamestown, Virginia, in 1619, against their will to propel slave owners' economic enterprise. They give details that the Atlantic slave trade led to a vast number of Africans being transported to America, put to grueling labor under the intimidation of horrid physical abuse, lynching, and dehumanizing in various ways by the slave master and his slave drivers. Abolitionist Frederick Douglass (1970, 81) in his second autobiography, *My Bondage and My Freedom*, depicts the slave's work, "From twelve o'clock (noon) till dark, the human cattle are in motion, wielding their clumsy hoes; turned on by no hope of reward, no sense of gratitude, no love of children; nothing, save the dread and terror of the slave driver's lash."

For example, the rhetoric in the *Willie Lynch Writings: Let's Make a Slave* describes how Black male slaves were treated differently than their female counterparts. These slaves were forbidden from assuming the traditional male gender roles. Male slaves performed hard labor and were subjected to harsh punishment. The *Willie Lynch Writings* suggests that slave owners used the same methods and tactics of breaking a horse to breaking the mental fortitude and physical prowess of Black male slaves. The document states:

> When it comes to breaking the uncivilized nigger, use the same process, but vary the degree and step up the pressure, so as to do a complete reversal of the mind. Take the meanest and most restless nigger, strip him of his clothes in front of the remaining male niggers, the female, and the nigger infant, tar and feather him, tie each leg to a different horse faced in opposite directions, set him afire and beat both horses to pull him apart in front of the remaining niggers. The next step is to take a bull-whip and beat the remaining nigger males to the point of death, in front of the female and the infant. Don't kill him, but put the fear of God in him, for he can be useful for future breeding. (Hassan-El 1999, 3)

As a result of the institutional and systemic structure of slavery, Black males were left in a vulnerable state of mind. The physical chains were removed; however, the mental psyche was destroyed. Gwen Bergner (1998) in her analysis of race suggests that the oppressive nature of the White male during slavery made him "the agent of a racist social order prohibiting Black males not only from satisfying sexual desire, but from achieving basic autonomy, normative masculinity, and self-determination" (253). Despite freeing the slaves, even Lincoln had a grim opinion on the plight of free Blacks. He states on September 18, 1858, during a campaign speech while running against Stephen A. Douglas of Illinois for a US Senate seat:

> I will say then that I am not, nor ever have been in favor of bringing about in anyway the social and political equality of the white and black races—that I am not nor ever have been in favor of making voters or jurors of negroes, nor of qualifying them to hold office, nor to intermarry with white people; and I will say in addition to this that there is a physical difference between the white and black races which I believe will forever forbid the two races living together on terms of social and political equality. And inasmuch as they cannot so live, while they do remain together there must be the position of superior and inferior, and

I as much as any other man am in favor of having the superior position assigned to the white race.[6]

On the one hand, the historical identity of the Black male is rooted in pain, suffering, and despair. On the other, it is also defined by achievements, triumphs, and victories. Most Black males are conscious of the oppressive society in which they live and understand that external and internal negative circumstances exist that will influence their cultural identity. In her work, Toby S. Jenkins (2006, 128) discusses the plight of Black males in American society:

> The challenges of reversing the negative circumstances facing African American men is daunting and requires working on the plight of the individual and transforming a broad array of social, political, economical, psychological, and educational issues that are deeply rooted in the very power structure of America. The challenge reflects a social oxymoron: seeking to advance the status of a population that the larger society has systematically oppressed.

This is similar to what W. E. B. DuBois (1903) in the first chapter of *The Souls of Black Folk* describes as a "double consciousness," which leads to a "warring soul." It is the warring ideal of having to subsist between White America and Black America in one dark body attempting to preserve both national and cultural identity. He writes, "One ever feels his twoness—an American, a Negro; two souls, two thoughts, two unreconciled strivings; two warring ideals in one dark body, whose dogged strength alone keeps it from being torn asunder" (45).

When DuBois formulated this theory in the early 1900s, Black identity in general depended mainly on the survival of being a Negro in White America. During this time, the ideal of being an American and Negro was perplexing in the eyes of Blacks who had only recently gained freedom. Further, DuBois writes, "The history of the American Negro is a history of this strife—this longing to attain self-conscious manhood, to merge his double self into a better and truer self" (45).

DuBois's use of the idea of "double consciousness" was groundbreaking in his exploration of race issues in the United States. His theory laid the foundation for a cultural landscape in Black America that could give the American Negro a sense of place and identity in White America. However, as Black Americans have become less of a homogenized group and exhibited a smaller amount of Black consciousness and solidarity since the twentieth century, the Black male identity has altered as well. Tekle Woldemikael (1989, 225) in his study of race consciousness suggests that two components have been viewed as essential to defining Black consciousness: "(1) accepting the racial identity and groupings of others on the basis of race; and (2) acting to redefine the inequality in status, privilege, and power between the two [main] racial groups." Because historical and current social experiences are largely responsible for the formation of Black consciousness, there is the belief that Black males should be able to build economic, social, and political institutions and continue a sense of group solidarity to assist in their structural, institutional, and individual plight.

The ideology of Black consciousness born out of slavery and fortified during the Civil Rights movement at one point in history led Black males to understand the importance of representing themselves as strong, righteous, promoters of collective action, and endearing to the Black community. That level of consciousness has diminished. Seldom now is the color of a Black male's skin a major factor that promotes loyalty, devotion, and pride to bond against economic, social, and political inequality, remnants of centuries of slavery and historical discrimination.

CURRENT BLACK MALE IDENTITY

For decades there has been a generational shift in the Black male identity. Much of this shift is attributed to the complex nature of the structural and cultural factors met head-on by Black males, which inevitably shapes their thinking and behavior. As talked about by William J. Wilson (2009) in *More than Just Race: Being Black and Poor in the Inner City*, structural factors such as joblessness, growing up and living in impoverished environments, and attending dilapidated public schools have a devastating effect on Black males. These structural factors coupled with cultural factors, such as exposure to drugs and gangs and being born into single female parent households, which leads to growing up without a father, shape the behavior of the current generation of young Black males.[7] The sum total of these negative factors triggers a daily assault on the Black male psyche and harmfully molds their cultural identity.

Negative factors have haunted the identity of Black males. Thus the election of President Obama initially was thought to invigorate and provide more opportunities for a Black male population that had experienced great hardship and despair. However, since he has been in office some structural and cultural factors have worsened. For example, Black male unemployment remains at record levels and job availability scarce. It ranged between 12 and 16 percent from 2009 to 2013 according to the US Department of Labor. In fact, in many large metropolitan cities, the Black male unemployment rate averaged close to or above 20 percent.[8]

Public schools have closed at an alarming rate during his presidency and laid off thousands of teachers, specifically in four majority Black cities: Chicago, Detroit, Philadelphia, and Washington, DC. Poor and minority children are being affected by failing school systems that have neglected the downturn of the American economy, slashing school budgets, and have received little economic support from state and national government. These two structural factors alone in many cases produce low-skilled and uneducated Black males who eventually commit crimes and become inmates in the prison industrial complex, which runs as an economic conglomerate that warehouses these males who succumb to these negative circumstances. According to a 2009 study conducted by the Pew Charitable Trusts titled "Collateral costs: Incarceration's effect on economic mobility," one out of three Black males (37.1 percent), ages 20–34, without a high school diploma or GED are imprisoned.[9]

Historically, tragic circumstances have prevailed in the lives of Black males. Despite this, many have found ways to overcome adversity. Some Black males have never been exposed to the structural and cultural liabilities that lead to a different cultural outcome. At the core of this discussion, we must acknowledge that a majority of young Black males need help to overcome these circumstances to be on the path to success and to flourish and become productive, hardworking individuals. However, the current autonomous Black male subculture, the failure of the adult Black population, and the "protest over politics" Black policy makers who have been ineffective in addressing issues germane to Black males (and the Black community as a whole) have led to redefining the Black male identity for better or worse in America.

To deconstruct the current Black male identity and gain a better understanding of their cultural identity, I began by asking the participants in this book, "What does it mean to be a Black male in the twenty-first century?" In reference to their cultural identity, three concerns emerged: (1) Black males felt that they were still thought of as "invisible" in White America; (2) the cultural identity of the Black male is often stripped to achieve the American Dream; and (3) there is a generational shift in Black male identity, especially among the younger generation.

The first theme that emerged was that many of the participants still felt "invisible." Sharoye, Banker, 42, expressed, "We are the single most overlooked group of people in all of society. In the words of [Ralph] Ellison we are still "Invisible Men." In his seminal book, *Invisible Man*, Ralph Ellison (1952) states:

> I am invisible. Misunderstood, simply because people refuse to see me.

> Like the bodiless heads you see sometimes in circus side-shows, it is as though I have been surrounded by mirrors of hard, distorting glass. When they approach me they see only my surroundings, themselves, or fragments of their imagination—indeed, everything and anything except me. (8)

A central point of emphasis in the book is that the narrator, the "Invisible Man," arrives at the realization that his identity comes from internal and external forces and it is incumbent upon him to adopt a moral balance to fight against racial elements in the world. The narrator continues to refer to himself as "Invisible." However, he develops a stronger identity while being faced with and overcoming challenges in life. Here some 60 years later Black males still struggle with feeling "socially invisible." There remains the challenge of converting stereotypes and elements of discrimination and racism into positive attributes and characteristics. Floyd, Entrepreneur, 47, expands on the notion of feeling "invisible":

> Imagine being told all your life that if you go to college and receive an education you will be accepted by White America. That will lead to you being able to overcome discrimination and stereotypes. You graduate, obtain employment at a well-known corporation and perform better than your White counterparts but don't receive any recognition for your work. That is what it feels like to be "invisible."

A vast number of participants who are college educated and hold professional careers share this same sentiment. Their views were disconcerting but understandable, as they have attempted to mirror mainstream society's perception of success, but struggled to gain outward and visible respect for their achievements. Many of them feel unappreciated in White American society. They are faced with the duality of having a "warring soul" as discussed above. Their focus is to work with the pressures and expectations of White America while maintaining their cultural identity. As scholar Elijah

Anderson (1997) notes, "So many of these blacks face the dual pressures and expectations of being 'professionals' in a white world" (115). Society has defined the criteria for success and labeled it as the "American Dream"—college-educated, lucrative job, home, married, children, and pet of choice. Once obtained, these criteria are somehow deemed insufficient in some circles. These Black males are now viewed as an exception to the rule rather than the norm; their achievements are relegated to being a novelty rather than a noteworthy accomplishment.

Another participant, Andre, Engineer, 46, added another quote from Ralph Ellison's *Invisible Man* to sum up his life experience:

> For, like almost everyone else in our country, I started out with my share of optimism. I believed in hard work and progress and action, but now, after first being "for" society and then "against" it, I assign myself no rank or any limit, and such an attitude is very much against the trend of the times. But my world has become one of infinite possibilities. (576)

The feeling of being "socially invisible" was not only exclusive to those with college degrees and professional careers. Even participants without degrees or who had lower-paying jobs had a similar response to the question. Oscar, Janitor, 62, expressed:

> I've seen a lot of things in my time on earth. America would have you to believe that there is a script you have to follow to become successful. That is not true. I'm proud of who I am and what I do. I know people walk past me everyday because the job I do is not glamorous. I've achieved the American Dream. And I didn't have to sellout to do it.

Greg, Plumber, 38 stated:

> I'm a strong, hardworking Black man. My father taught me the value of hard work. I don't have a degree. But I provide for my

family. We don't live off the [welfare] system. I have a good life.

False Black Male Identity

This analysis goes beyond the traditional paradigm in exploring Black male identity and argues that a specific segment of Black males no longer considers negative stereotypes and labels offensive unless they are inferred by Whites. As I have identified the structural and cultural factors faced by Black males that shape their identity, an emerging self-identity is manifesting itself among the younger generation of Black males: *Real Nigga*. This self-label is not germane to a specific cultural environment, geographical location, socioeconomic status, social class, or those in single-parent households. It begins in the adolescent age range and spans over age categories. While it is valuable to the discourse to dissect the identity of all age ranges of Black males, the central focus in this section needs and must be on the younger generation of Black males who have adopted a false Black male identity.

Huge pools of younger Black males are becoming more disconnected from mainstream society. They have adopted a street code that has distanced them from the rest of America. This degree of alienation has led some to develop a certain mentality and way of living, a "I'm a real nigga, I don't give a fuck" attitude per se, which liberates them and allows this specific population of young Black males to subsist in American society. One of the younger participants, Harold, Warehouse Worker, 22, states:

> I'm a real nigga. That's what it means to be [a] Black [male] in the twenty-first century. We [Black males] out here every day in these streets trying to make ends meet. I'm hustlin' and working to try to make it. I would have went to school but I know plenty of school folks making less than me. You heard the song, *Amerika*, by Trick Daddy, you got "4 degrees and a Ph.D./ still a nigga."/

Before I fully discuss this emerging term, "real nigga," it is essential to talk about the term "nigga," which preceded it and has been at the center of racial controversy between Blacks and Whites for decades. Much has been written about and discussed related to this term. Since its inception, the term "nigger" has been used among Whites and directed toward Blacks as a racial epithet. On the other hand, the term "nigga" is also commonly used among some Blacks as a term of endearment. The visceral hate embodied in the legacy of this term coupled with its divisiveness in the Black community sparked a substantial discussion among the participants in this book.

In 1997, the National Association for the Advancement of Colored People (NAACP) led at the time by Kweisi Mfume requested that *Merriam-Webster's Collegiate Dictionary* revise its definition of the term "nigger." The ninth and tenth editions defined "nigger" as:

1. a black person—usually taken to be offensive.
2. a member of any dark-skinned race—usually taken to be offensive.
3. a member of a socially disadvantaged class of persons.

During this time, Frederick C. Mish, *Webster's* editor-in-chief, argued that the definition reflected the common usage of the term. Based on *Webster's* definition, one could paint a portrait of a "nigger" as all those who are Black, poor, and from a socially disadvantaged environment. *Webster's* racial approval of the term sparked controversy from the NAACP and other civil rights groups of its open usage.

To the dismay of many civil rights leaders, in today's Black culture the term "nigger" has been deracialized and stripped of its negative connotation by rap artists, comedians, writers, and those in the Black community who have changed the spelling to "nigga" believing the term is not as racially charged as in the past. Blacks in the past have been described by racial bigots with such derogatory terms as Coon, Spook,

Sambo, Uncle Tom, Tar Baby, Colored, Porch Monkey, and a host of others. However, the term "nigger" has always remained a constant.

In his stimulating book *Nigger: The Strange Career of a Troublesome Word*, Professor Randall Kennedy (2002) believes that the term "nigger is fascinating precisely because it has been put to a variety of uses and can radiate a wide array of meanings" (34). First, there is the "nigger" versus "nigga" examination. I believe the terms "nigger" and "nigga" should have no distinctive difference in their meanings. The term "nigga" is an offshoot of "nigger," which as stated is now commonly used in the Black community as a term of endearment. For example, "what's up nigga?" or "that is my nigga" are phrases that are supposed to exemplify positive connotations. In 2006, Black political leaders such as US Rep. Maxine Waters, D-California, Rev. Jesse Jackson, Rev. Al Sharpton, and Comedian Paul Mooney, famed for using the term "nigga" in his standup comedy acts, launched a national campaign for Blacks in entertainment to stop using the N-word.

Second, there is the debate of the excessive use of the term "nigga" in rap songs. Opponents of rap music speculate that the lyrical content in some songs have gone too far. They argue that the content is too misogynistic, violent, rebels against American values, and more importantly, uses some variation of the term "nigga/s/z" too much. This reinforces negative stereotypes and labeling of Black males. Table 1.1, for instance, counts the number of times Grammy-winning rap artist Lil Wayne has used the terms "nigga/s/z" and "real nigga/s/z" in his ten studio albums from 1999 to 2013. He has uttered some variation of the terms "nigga/s/z" approximately 1,028 and "real nigga/s/z" 21 times.[10] If a young Black male (or young White male for that matter) grows up as a Lil Wayne fan, there is no doubt that the repetitiveness of listening to him use this term will have some impact on that individual's tendency to use the term even as slang.

Table 1.1   Lil Wayne's Usage of the N-Word, 1999–2013

Albums	"Nigga/s/z"	"Real Nigga/s/z"	Total
Tha Block Is Hot (1999)	188	3	191
Lights Out (2000)	181	1	182
500 Degreez (2002)	71	0	71
Tha Carter (2004)	123	9	132
Tha Carter II (2005)	82	0	82
The Leak EP (2007)	28	0	28
(5 songs)			
Tha Carter III (2008)	23	0	23
(Grammy, Best Rap Album)			
I Am Not A Human Being (2010)	48	1	49
Tha Carter IV (2011)	98	5	103
I Am Not A Human Being II (2013)	186	2	188
Total #	1,028	21	1,049

Note: The above table contains the total number of times Lil Wayne used the term "nigga/s/z" and "real nigga/s/z" in his ten solo albums for the given years. This chart does not include the count from studio songs with the rap group Hot Boyz (1996–2001), mixtapes with rap group The Sqad (1999–2003), his duo album with Birdman titled *Like Father, Like Son* (2006), solo mixtapes, or song features. In addition, the table only counts when Lil Wayne uses the terms in the songs even when other artists are featured on the song.

From the years 2005 to 2010, Lil Wayne was arguably considered the best rapper in the world and continues to be a household name in the rap industry. Looking at table 1.1, as a 17-year-old at the beginning of his solo career in 1999, he used the term excessively. During the height of his rap career from 2005 to 2010 while recording four albums, he used some variation of the term "nigga/s/z" only a total of 181 times. Specifically during the recording of *Tha Carter III* (2008), which won a Grammy for Best Rap Album and sold nearly 2.9 million albums by the end of 2008, he used the N-word a mere 23 times. However, at the age of 30, in 2013, with the recording of his tenth solo album, *I Am Not A Human Being II*, he returned to his excessive usage of the N-word uttering it 186 times.

Fans of rap music, Black and White, ages 16–30, are the group most likely to consume the music (Smith 2005). It is clear that some have become desensitized to the term while others may be cognitively influenced by the repetition of the terms and believe this to be part of their self-identity. These terms are committed to memory and repeated unconsciously. Some Black males in this age range are unaware of the historical context of the term "nigga." Therefore, the underlying lyrical messages being narrated in the songs that encompass these terms carry no merit for them.

Many young listeners of rap music were not born during its formation in New York in the early 1970s and are unaware of the social consciousness era of the art form. According to Berry and Looney (1996, 266), when speaking of rap during its early days, "rap music has reintroduced Black identity and consciousness." Early groups such as Grandmaster Flash and the Furious Five with songs such as *The Message* (1982) and political groups such as Public Enemy, Clan X, Poor Righteous Teachers and others pioneered a conscious rap movement in the mid-1980s. Hip-hop scholar Nelson George in his book *Hip-Hop America* (1998) describes the early days of hip-hop music as "a product of post-civil rights era America" (viii). One hip-hop enthusiast, Aaron, Lawyer, 28, expresses:

> I love hip-hop music; the old and new. But the excessive use of "nigga" is becoming a turnoff for me. I want to hear lyrical content that has a message not "nigga this" or "nigga that" every couple of words. Using the N-word does not validate an artist's existence. What's the point of saying the N-word a lot of times in a song? Real hip-hop is dead.

The multiple functions of the N-word and its mainstay in the hip-hop culture lead us to explore the birth of the term "real nigga." Besides hearing the term in rap songs, in general it is now commonplace in the Black community to hear males refer to themselves as "real niggas." For instance, you may hear a Black male describe himself in the following capacity, "I'm a real nigga." They use this term as if it provides them with an identity. But missing from the acknowledgment of this term among Blacks males is its meaning. What does it mean to be a "real nigga?" How do we define this term and provide it with a proper context? As stated, Black males have deracialized the term "nigga," but now add an elusive adjective to further embrace a historically damaging racial epithet. Is "real nigga" the new Black male identity? And does it characterize life in some Black male subcultures?

One explanation for the embrace of this variation of the N-words can be found in Elijah Anderson's (1999) book, *Code of the Streets*, whereby he discusses how mutual honor and respect within a subculture, particularly among Black males, brings about an unwritten code and ascribes a separate language among the members. Those who assert themselves within this subculture must display specific characteristics such as aggression and willingness to defend themselves, which is essential for formulating an identity among their peers and for gaining respect. There are forces, like the presence of strong Black males, that could potentially offset negative influences such as joining gangs, selling drugs, and committing crimes. However, the absence of fathers and such figures in the community pressures young Black males to adopt the code of the street as a survival mechanism. It is important to develop a social identity in the community, one in line with the subculture—a set of informal rules that governs the behavior of Black males. Knowledge of the code is necessary to be able to function and survive in the environment. Applied to Black males in subcultures that address themselves as "real niggas," this interpersonal dialogue is needed for those having to handle themselves in a street-oriented environment. Hip-hop scholar Jeffery O. G. Ogbar (2007) in the introduction to his book, *Hip-Hop Revolution*, provides a narrow definition of "real nigga." He states, "Fundamentally, a 'real nigga' refers to a tough urban black male who is intimately familiar with and willing to confront the many challenges of the 'hood'" (6).

On the contrary, some Black males do not come from non-supportive environments, nor are they participants in deviant activities. Scholar Robin Kelley (1994) states in his book, *Race Rebels*, "the experiences of young black men in the inner city are not universal to all black people" (210). But yet, why do Black males from affluent environments also refer to themselves as "real niggas"? The logical answer is that they have grown up in the hip-hop culture and as a result many have adopted the terms "nigga" and "real nigga" as daily references. One participant, Kyren, Railroad Conductor, 35, explains, "Dudes use 'nigga' and 'real nigga' as slang. Nothing more, nothing less."

His retort begs the question even more intensely, what does it mean to be a "real nigga" in America? Soliciting the responses of some of the participants, I asked them to define the term "real nigga."

> Ashton, Student, 19: Real nigga—Is someone who can hold their own; mentally, physically and financially. It is someone who makes themselves and the people around them better.
>
> Cameron, Student, 21: Real nigga—A person that is true to his word. He keeps it 100 [%]. A nigga that is loyal and committed to his niggas.
>
> Anthony, Social Worker, 35: Real nigga—Trustworthy, hardworker, honest and true to his family and friends. Educated whether it be in the classroom, streets or both; Respect and take care of his people. He is comfortable in his own skin.

These definitions clearly show that some Black males have adopted this term in a positive, endearing connation that exhibits loyalty and honor among each other. In contrast, there are those who despise the term and view it as harshly as "nigga." One of the participants, Jade, Personal Trainer, 30, explained:

> I personally define it as a disgrace. Yes, some may use it as a badge of honor or as a way to take "control" of the word and make it their own. But in reality, many died and sacrificed their

lives to terminate the word and everything it stands for. You wouldn't hear Dr. [Martin Luther] King refer to himself as a "real nigga."

John, Maintenance Worker, 39, uttered his disdain for the term:

I guess in order to be considered a "real nigga" it is important for these dudes to be authentic about their exchanges with others in the Black community to validate their street credibility. A "real nigga" may witness a crime and withhold information from law enforcement for fear of being labeled as a "snitch." Withholding that information is a form of "keeping it real." Even if his best friend is killed. That is stupid.

Rap artist Hopsin makes an attempt to define the term "real nigga" in his 2012 mixtape song, *Ill Mind of Hopsin 5*:

The term "real nigga's" publicly used/ And I need to know what it means, cause I'm fuckin' confused/ Are you one for always busting your tool/ With nothing to lose and something to prove to homies up in your crew/

He later raps in the next verse:

A real nigga don't brag about being real as long as he knows it/ And his future doesn't seem hopeless/ A real nigga stays out of jail, handles shit, and he keeps focused/

In contrast to the previous definitions, Hopsin identifies the negative connotations of the term. His rap verse coincides with Elijah Anderson's cultural perspective that pinpoints specific attributes such as carrying guns, having an "I don't give a fuck" attitude, selling drugs, and hustling, all of which are a part of a street culture mentality.

Exploring the term "real nigga" has brought out a range of definitions. With the information provided it is possible to simply deduce that the term means different things to different people. Thus it is reasonable to conclude that the core of the term "nigga" and its behavioral response among Black males is still mixed. As Ogbar (2007, 7) concludes, "that definition, however, is in flux." But to add "real" to the term further exhibits the debatable usage. The addition of "real" somehow implies that there is an extraordinary element to being a "nigga," an identity that some young Black males of this generation are unfortunately more than happy to take on.

The logical conclusion is that the terms "nigga" and "real nigga" were born out of a dysfunctional psychological and social condition created in certain subcultures among Black males and were also fed by artists in the hip-hop culture who excessively use the term in their songs to validate their street credibility. Structural and cultural forces never allowed some of these males to develop a "sense of self," which would in no way entice them to refer to themselves as "real niggas." The trend is recent and still ambiguous; however, it is creating a shift in the cultural identity of young Black males who believe that the self-label of "real nigga" validates their male existence.

CONCLUSION

In this chapter I have looked at the Black male identity. Past history along with current structural and cultural factors have shaped the cultural identity of Black males. Despite the strong historical lineage of Black males who grew up facing injustices, overcame them, and paved the way for economic, social, and political advancement, some members of this generation are experiencing a "crisis of identity." Even as this chapter voices the sentiments of Black males who have achieved success but still feel "socially invisible" and that their cultural identity is often stripped in an attempt to achieve the American Dream, the flip side is that a younger generation of Black males has disregarded institutionally and socially constructed forces that have shaped the identity of an older generation of Black males, and they view themselves differently. While we question the ascribed labels and their outlook on certain elements of life, much is to be said about a generation of Black males who believe it is imperative to pave their own path and redefine what it means to be a Black male in America.

The positive and negative implications of the Black male identity warrant continual discourse. From President Obama, to the typical young striving Black male to a Black male who consumes his day smoking marijuana and playing video games, it is difficult to deconstruct the Black male identity. As evident in this chapter the Black male identity has contrasting and competing forces that are played out in the annals of American society. The deconstruction of the Black male identity will remain an arduous task as their identity continues to evolve.

CHAPTER 2

We All Came from a Woman: Rap Music and Misogyny

In her important book, *Black Noise* (1994), hip-hop scholar Tricia Rose defines rap music as, "a black cultural expression that prioritizes black voices from the margins of urban America" (2). The genre of rap music that escalated to national prominence in the early 1970s has endured many artistic transformations. Born from the hip-hop culture, rap music has grown into many distinctive sub-genres. During the late 1980s and early 1990s, the most publicized of these was "gangsta rap." This subgenre has been a voice for Black urban youth that draw from rap as a medium to express frustrations about historic racial injustice, economic deprivation, police repression, and violence in their communities.

Nestled in gangsta rap and other subgenres are misogynist lyrics that degrade and objectify women. Terri M. Adams and Douglas B. Fuller (2006) define misogyny in gangsta rap as the "promotion, glamorization, support, humorization, justification, or normalization of oppressive ideas about women" (940). They argue that the misogynist content in different subgenres of rap music mimics society. Therefore, "misogyny in its varied forms does not exist in a vacuum but is instead a part of a larger social, cultural, and economic system that sustains and perpetuates the ideology" (941). Some Black male rap artists carelessly use lyrics of an oppressive nature worsening gender inequality in society.

The negative portrayal of Black women in rap music has received increased academic attention since the mid-1990s. Early scholars such as Wade and Thomas-Gunner (1993), Took and Weiss (1994), Barongan and Hall (1995), Johnson, Jackson, and Gatto (1995), and Johnson, Adams, Ashburn, and Reed (1995) found that misogynist and violent rap lyrics do promote greater acceptance of the use of violence against women. Hip-hop scholars who have continued this line of research have focused their attention on how misogynist lyrics influence young rap music listeners' attitude and behavior toward women. This research focus has since contributed to fueling additional studies (e.g., Armstrong 2001; Adams and Fuller 2006; Cobb and Boettcher 2007; Weitzer and Kubrin 2009; Gourdine and Lemmons 2011).

Given rap music is one of the more popular genres among youth today (Smith 2005), studies continue to appear that dissect misogynistic messages in the lyrics. Many of these songs contain lyrics about the sexual assault and rape of women and further promote "models of masculinity that sustain and encourage misogyny" (Cobb and Boettcher 2007, 3026). This chapter opens dialogue on rap songs that contain the misogynistic message of sexual assault and rape because several major themes became apparent in interviews with Black male participants. They believed authentic rap music has "died," boasts too much about "material" items (e.g., cars, jewelry, and popping bottles in the club), and contains "degrading" lyrics that demean women and celebrate rape. Jermaine, Former Professional Athlete, 41, believed, "The current state of rap music is in shambles. Young men only talk about selling drugs, smoking weed, popping bottles and raping women. It's counterproductive to the plight of Black men. I don't want my son doing either of those things. Especially not raping women." According to Adams and Fuller (2006, 940), misogynist rap lyrics diminish the status of women to sexual objects, "that are only good for sex and abuse and are ultimately a burden to men." Additionally, scholars such as Armstrong (2001) and Weitzer and Kubrin

(2009) have identified impressionable misogynistic messages in their research. These messages range from derogatory name-calling of women (e.g., bitches and hoes), violence against women, prostitution, and pimping, to sexual assault and rape.

The objective of this chapter is to increase our understanding about the nature and consequences of a Black male–dominated music genre that in some cases is being used as a medium to present the misogynistic message of sexual assault and rape. Are such misogynistic messages in rap songs a reflection of Black masculinity? Is there in fact a connection between the lyrical messages of Black male rap artists and the actions of Black male consumers? It is argued among scholars that Black masculinity is fixed to rap music. Therefore, aside from the past role rap music has provided in uplifting Black males, dialogue among participants is critical in comprehending its proliferation as a music genre that now promotes and embraces misogynistic messages.

Misogynistic Message of Sexual Assault and Rape

Since its inception, rap music has been a Black male–dominated music genre. Rap artists have presented misogynistic messages in lyrics and videos that have objectified women and perpetuated gender oppression. Social critics have argued that when artists' songs contain misogynistic lyrics that promote violence against women, the distinction between the actual lyrics and intention of the lyrics often is blurred. Is rap music simply a by-product of a society that condones sexual exploitation of women? Or should Black male artists be held more accountable for their demeaning lyrics and lewd imagery in videos? Alvin, Contractor, 29, was asked what he believes is the current state of rap music, "Honestly, I'm not a fan of rap music anymore. It's the same message in every song—I'm a real nigga, pop bottles, smoke weed, fuck hoes, I need a bad bitch, etc. I have a daughter now. I don't want her to listen to it nor do I play it in the car." Along the same lines, Bernard, Minister, 47, argued, "Rap music is a disgrace to the Black community. I'm disappointed in the direction of rap music. It used to be feel good music. I was a big fan of the Sugarhill Gang. But when gangsta rappers like Schoolly D, Ice T, Ice Cube, Snoop [Dogg] and others came into the game it went down. I was a huge fan of rap music before they talked about killing each other and degrading Black women."

In the early 1990s, gangsta rap music that was already under a national microscope for its violent messages drew more criticism for its excessive usage of derogatory terms such as "bitches" and "hoes" and explicit references to "rape" in the lyrics. It became littered with profane references to Black women that branded and objectified them. Bakari Kitwana (2002, 87), a former executive editor for the hip-hop magazine *The Source*, expresses in his book *The Hip-Hop Generation*, "The very misogynist, antagonistic depictions of young Black women in a music form dominated by young Black males reflect the extent of the tension brewing between young Black men and women." In essence, some elements of rap music serve as a gross misrepresentation of Black masculinity and undermine the Black male-female relationship. Equally disturbing in the quest for Black males to be held more accountable for their lyrical content is that many female listeners entertain songs that contain such lyrics.

The misogynistic message of sexual assault and rape in rap songs is not as excessive, but seems to carry greater societal implications. Vonn, Educator, 26, voiced his concern with such messages when describing an incident at his place of employment. He stated:

> One morning after homeroom I was assigned to safety patrol. My job was to roam the hallways and make sure students were attending class. I heard noises coming from the bathroom. I entered [the bathroom] to find two boys had pushed a girl into the stall and were trying to convince her to have sex with them. When I met with each of them one-on-one to inquire about

the incident, one of the boys told me he was just doing what he heard in the song, *Take The Pussy*. I asked him where had he heard the song. His reply was "my older brother listens to it all the time."

The 1992 song *Take The Pussy* is from the defunct rap group Too Much Trouble based in Houston, Texas. The group consisted of four members, three Black and one White. In the first verse, the lone White member, Bar-None, raps:

I ain't gonna pay for shit that I can take/ And I love it when a bitch screams rape/

Each verse in the song depicts a graphic scene of raping a woman who refuses to willingly submit to a man's sexual desires.

The extent to which misogynistic messages have a negative societal impact is the focus of many of the above studies. Despite the fact that a number of studies suggest a connection between misogynistic messages and aggressive and violent attitudes among males, few empirical studies have included the misogynistic message of sexual assault and rape. While this chapter does not posit that there is a direct correlation between rap music and the sexual assault and rape of women, without question misogynistic messages express negative attitudes and opinions about women. According to Pierre, Social Worker, 42, "The music tells them what to do. If it says "kill," they kill; if it says "rob," they rob; if it says "rape," they probably will believe it is ok to rape. Black males are not absolved from sexual assault. In my line of work, I see young Black males that are offenders of sexual assault everyday. I can't say the music makes them do it. But, I bet if you trace rap music to the early days when rappers started talking about rape, you'll find a pattern."

During the late 1980s and early 1990s, mainstream rap artists and groups began to use the misogynistic message of sexual assault and rape in their songs. In 1989, the Geto

Boys, another rap group based in Houston, Texas, released the song *Mind of a Lunatic*, wherein member Bushwick Bill raps the following:

> She's naked, and I'm a peeping tom/ Her body's beautiful, so I'm thinking rape/ Shouldn't have had her curtains open, so that's her fate/

The content in this song drew harsh criticism from women's groups and protestors, as many believed it celebrated sexual violence against women. This period in rap music pushed the envelope of vile and degrading sexual lyrics.

In 1993, rap icon Tupac Shakur released *Keep Ya Head Up*, which in stark contradiction was a song intended to empower Black women. He raps:

> And since we all came from a woman/ Got our name from a woman and our game from a woman/ I wonder why we take from our women/ Why we rape our women/ Do we hate our women?/

Tupac's lyrics were a departure from the types of songs that dominated the mid-1980s and '90s. Despite his plea to Black males in the song to empower Black females, he too often objectified women in other songs. On the one hand, he could make empowering songs like *Keep Ya Head Up, Brenda's Got a Baby, Dear Mama,* and *Changes* and on the other he also made *How Do U Want It* and *All About U*, which demeaned women. On November 18, 1993, Tupac was accused and later convicted of raping Ayanna Jackson, a Black woman, at the Le Parker Meridien Hotel. She alleged that Tupac and three other men raped and sodomized her. Just four days prior she had performed oral sex on Tupac at a nightclub. He was eventually found guilty and sentenced to two and a half years in prison. During the court proceedings, Tupac vehemently denied the sexual assault allegations. Also in 1993, Grammy award–winning rap group Bone Thugs-n-Harmony (then known as B.O.N.E. Enterpri$e), at the beginning of their career, released the song *Def Dick*. Krayzie Bone, one of the popular members of the group, raps:

> And once the def dicks on the loose/ So bitch you can't escape/
> So hold this feelin, cause if you don't, I'm thinkin' rape/

Legendary New York rapper, the Notorious B.I.G. (aka Biggie Smalls), had several songs during his career that contained references to rape. In the 1994 song, *Just Playing (Dreams)*, he raps, "You can 76 the 69, try 68/ Make Raven-Symoné call date rape/ Only cause I'm paid." At the time Raven-Symoné, born December 10, 1985, was only nine years old. In 1997, the Notorious B.I.G. recites in the song *What's Beef?*:

> Don't they know my nigga Gutter fuckin' kidnap kids?/ Fuck
> 'em in the ass, throw 'em over the bridge/

These lyrics represent a disgusting portrayal of sexual assault against young males. During the time of this song, social critics suggested that the Notorious B.I.G.'s lyrics closely referenced the late 1970s and early 1980s Atlanta Child Murders. Beginning in the summer of 1979 till spring of 1981 more than two dozen Black males were killed in Atlanta, Georgia. Some of their bodies were discarded in rivers in the Atlanta metropolitan area.

One of the most heinous references to rape in a rap song came in 1998. On his debut album, *It's Dark and Hell Is Hot*, rap artist DMX (aka Dark Man X) makes an explicit reference to statutory rape and murder in the song *X is Coming*. He raps:

> I'm comin in the house and I'm gunnin' for your spouse/ Tryin'
> to send the bitch back to her maker/ And if you got a daughter
> older than 15, I'm a rape her/

DMX clearly describes a violent scenario that involves the sexual assault of a teenage female. The vile lyrics in the song received limited negative criticism. Moreover, the album *It's Dark and Hell Is Hot* debuted at number one on the billboard charts, received positive acclaim, and has sold more than five million copies worldwide.

Since 1998, many rap artists have made explicit references to rape in their songs. Table 2.1 shows the recent cases from 2009 to 2013 (see table 2.1). It displays the names of artist, title of songs, and rape-specific rap lyrics. The latest artist to offer controversial rap lyrics in a song is multiplatinum rapper Rick Ross. In 2013 he came under public scrutiny for his verse on artist Rocko's song *U.O.E.N.O.* that seems to celebrate rape. He raps:

> Put Molly all in her champagne, she ain't even know it/ I took her home and I enjoyed that, she ain't even know it/

Shortly after the release of the song it was criticized for condoning rape. Criticism mounted from women's groups that Ross had crossed the line of not only making reference to rape but also unknowingly slipping a synthetic drug, Molly, in a woman's drink that would act as a date rape drug. His initial response to the criticism was aired on the New Orleans radio station Q93 in which he indicated the lyrics were a "misunderstanding" and the term "rape" was not used in the song. Ross's denial about the severity of the rape reference led to more backlash and also the loss of major endorsement deals. He later offered an official apology. In the statement, Ross wrote:

> Before I am an artist, I am a father, a son, and a brother to some of the most cherished women in the world. So for me to suggest in any way that harm and violation be brought to a woman is one of my biggest mistakes and regrets...most recently, my choice of words was not only offensive, it does not reflect my true heart. And for this, I apologize...To the young men who listen to my music, please know that using a substance to rob a woman of her right to make a choice is not only a crime, it's wrong and I do not encourage it.[1]

Table 2.1 Rape References in Rap Music, 2009–2013

Artist(s)	Song	Year	Lyrics
Rocko featuring Rick Ross	U.O.E.N.O	2013	Rick Ross: *Put Molly all in her champagne, she ain't even know it/ I took her home and I enjoyed that, she ain't even know it/*
Freddie Gibbs	187 Proof	2012	*You know who you fucking with? A nigga who got shit to lose/ I got niggas that rob you and rape yo bitch if they in the mood/*
Vado	We Outchea	2012	*Never fucked, nut you ate that/ My niggas fucked and we raped that/*
Big L featuring Cam'ron and Bloodshed	Harlem Nights	2012	Bloodshed:*Murder astrologist, mad cases of manslaughter/ I rape this man's daughter, then put the shit on camcorder/*
N.O.R.E. featuring Pusha T and Meek Mill	Scared Money	2011	Meek Mill: *If I ever go broke, I'm a take yo money/ Have my nigga snatch yo bitch and rape yo honey/*
Big L	Devil's Son	2010	*It's Big L and I'm all about taking funds/ I'm a stone villain known for killing and raping nuns/*
Tech N9ne featuring KrizzKaliko and Craig Smith (Remix)	Liked I Died	2010	KrizzKaliko: *Raped a Vegas hooker, told her pimp he should pay me/ At O.J.'s house and creepin' out with his Lady/*
Rick Ross featuring Gunplay	Gunplay	2009	Rick Ross: *Tellin' lies gettin' niggas wives tied up and raped/*
Tyga	Ice Cream Paintjob (freestyle)	2009	*Money ain't a thing to the Young Money gang baby/ Our Navy, RA and even rape your lady/*
Tyler The Creator	Blow	2009	*You call this shit kids, well I call these kids cum/ And you call this shit rape but I think that rape's fun/*

Note: Rap artist Eminem has two songs that make explicit references to rape: (1) From his 2009 album, *Relapse*, in the song *Stay Wide Awake* and (2) On Lloyd Banks's 2010 album, *The Hunger for More 2*(H.F.M.2), in the song *Celebrity*.

The Rick Ross incident was the first of its kind to gain this type of national media exposure. Hip-hop critics suggest that the objectification of women is commonplace and cases such as Rick Ross's are only highlighted when the rapper has mainstream popularity. The following questions surface: Has a "rape culture" become normalized in the music genre of rap music? Are the lyrics telling young Black males that sexual assault and rape is acceptable? Hip-hop scholar Jeffery O. G. Ogbar (2007, 73) suggests, "[rap music's] hypermasculine style has been blamed for much of the contemptuous expression directed at women."

RACE AND RAPE

Statistics from the Bureau of Justice Statistics' (BJS) National Crime Victimization Survey (NCVS) and Federal Bureau of Investigation's Uniform Crime Reports (UCR), show an alarming pattern of Black males sexually assaulting and raping women. When these statistics were conveyed to participants, many dismissed them as "the White man is always trying to get us." Marlon, Carpenter, 52, articulated, "For centuries, there has been a belief that Black males were rapist. White men made up that bullshit. They wanted White women to fear Black men. This was long before rap music. I agree that there may be a problem nowadays. Let's not blame rap music. Rap music cannot make these young men rape."

The crimes of sexual assault and rape are primarily male dominated and intraracial. By far the greatest myth in examining the criminality of Black males is that they mainly rape White women (Wyatt 1992). This myth is rooted in slavery and has persisted till date. Scott J. South and Richard B. Felson (1990, 87) in their study of racial patterns of rape argued that, "black rapists are no more likely to choose a white woman than white rapists are to choose a black [woman]."

Despite attitudes about race and rape being built on racial myths and fears, Black males disproportionately make up the assailants in rape cases. The 2011 UCR reported that Blacks represented 32.9 percent of arrestees for forcible rape compared to 65 percent for Whites. Blacks under 18 years represented 36.5 percent of rape assailants.[2] According to Gary D. LaFree (1982) in a longitudinal study of interracial rape spanning a 45-year-period, he found that Blacks were arrested for rape an average of 6.52 times more often than Whites. While much of this disparity can historically be attributed to racial myths, profiling, and hoax, there is an underlying concern based on available data that young Black males are participating in more crimes that involve sexual assault and rape. As stated by Innis, Educator, 34, "It's a culmination of factors that motivate these young men to participate in these acts. The statistics speak volumes. We can blame the child, the parents, the schools, etc. However, some blame needs to be on the culture. Rap music is embedded in the Black culture. I listen to Black male students rap about nonsense all day. Many believe what they are rapping about to be the truth. The lyrics in the songs are like instructions to them. The sad part is that Black females are the victims of their actions."

The NCVS reported in 2012 that the rate of sexual assaults and rapes had increased. Approximately 346,830 Americans were victims. Only 28 percent of total sexual assaults and rapes were reported to law enforcement. This type of victimization is the least reported of all violent crimes. The causes for low reporting range from fear, little confidence that the attacker will be brought to justice, to the double victimization of having to relive the experience when explaining to law enforcement officials or in court proceedings. Even less victims (8.2 percent) received assistance from public and private agencies that support individuals in their emotional and physical recovery from these types of crimes.[3]

The 2010 NCVS, which has a demographic breakup by race and gender, reported that 55.4 percent of Black women compared to 52.4 percent of White women were victims of violent crimes. Proportionally, Black women are victims of violent crimes more than any other racial and ethnic minority group. Nearly one in five Black women (22 percent) at some point in their lives will become victims of rape.[4] Such national reports as NCVS and UCR show that Black women are less likely than White women to report acts of sexual assault and rape. For every Black woman that reports her rape, at least 15 do not report to law enforcement officials. This has created a "culture of silence" among Black women. Studies suggest that Black women are less likely to report cases because it contributes to sexual stereotypes about them and feeds existing racial myths of Black men. Gail E. Wyatt (1992), in her examination of the outcome differences of Black and White female victims of rape, found that Black women were significantly more likely than White women to be blamed for their rape. She also found that Black women, more than their White counterparts, tend to be victims of repeated sexual assaults.

It is plausible that rap artists whose songs contain the misogynistic message of sexual assault and rape are unaware of the rate of these crimes against Black women. Yet, if they were aware would their consciousness weigh more heavily toward being accountable in their lyrical content than having misogynistic content in their songs in an attempt to gain commercial success? Do they realize the effect their lyrics have on the younger generation of Black males? Bruce H. Wade and Cynthia A. Thomas-Gunner (1993), in their study of the effect of rap lyrics on the attitudes of Black college students, found that Black males "agreed that rap [music] accurately reflects at least some of the reality of gender relations between black males and females" (58). Males who preferred listening to songs that contained misogynistic messages had significantly more rape-prone attitudes.

In many ways rap music affirms the gender oppression that has haunted Black women since slavery. As female activist Angela Y. Davis (1993, 34) notes in her work on Black feminism, "Great art never achieves its greatness through an act of absolute transcendence of socio-historical reality. On the contrary, even as it transcends specific circumstances, it is deeply rooted in social realities." While materialistic messages and derogatory name-calling toward women are deemed as acceptable among rap artists, misogynistic messages that encourage sexual assault and rape rightfully should be at the center of public scrutiny. Such misogynistic messages warrant intensive discourse. At its most fundamental level, rap music surfaced to empower Black people as a whole, not only to empower Black males and oppress Black females further to promote gender inequality.

Survey of Black College Students

One of the primary tasks in this chapter is to increase our understanding of how the misogynistic message of sexual assault and rape influences the behavior of Black males. To do so, a baseline survey was administered to a convenient sample of Black undergraduate students at a Midwestern University to determine whether or not rap songs that contain the misogynistic message of sexual assault and rape shape their attitudes (see Appendix A.2). Black males and females were placed in two groups, an experimental group and a control group. Prior to the survey, the experimental group was asked to: (1) read an educational brochure on sexual assault and rape; (2) listen to rap artist DMX's *X Is Coming*, which contains the misogynistic message of statutory rape; and (3) view rap artist Nelly's video *Tip Drill*, a sexually explicit video that is deemed to exploit and objectify females. The control group was asked to watch feminist rap artist Queen Latifah's video *Ladies First*, whose lyrics and image is intended to empower females, and then perform the survey.

First, participants in the experimental group were provided with an educational brochure on sexual assault and rape. The brochure outlined the types of abuses ranging from dating violence, emotional and verbal abuse, stalking, to sexual assault and date rape, and provided statistical information on the rate of sexual assaults and rapes on college campuses, coping mechanisms for females in their healing and recovery, and information about crisis hotlines and centers that specialize in helping victims.

Second, they listened to rap artist DMX's song *X Is Coming*. Released in 1998, many participants did not have a reference of this rap song. Due to its vile content and the limited negative criticism during this period, it was suitable to introduce it to the experimental group. It contains not only the misogynistic message of statutory rape but also other offensive and violent messages that are projected in the song. Participants listened to the song and were provided with a copy of the lyrics for the entire song. Consider the focal lyrics of the song:

> I'm comin in the house and I'm gunnin' for your spouse/ Tryin' to send the bitch back to her maker/ And if you got a daughter older than 15, I'm a rape her/

Third, these experimental group members were asked to watch rap artist Nelly's video *Tip Drill*. The phrase *Tip Drill* is a slang term often used to refer to a promiscuous female. In 2003, the video sparked controversy as female college students and womens groups protested its contents. It renewed the discussion of the denigration of Black females in rap videos. Nelly, who was scheduled to perform at Spelman College in Atlanta, Georgia, canceled his scheduled appearance after students argued that his video portrayed Back women in a negative light. The video is filled with half-naked women in different suggestive scenes such as stripping, simulating a ménage à trois, and exhibiting bisexuality. For instance, in one scene Nelly is shown swiping a credit card between a woman's derrière. Women are depicted throughout the video as hypersexualized props and sexual objects. The lyrics paint a similar picture. Members of the rap group St. Lunatics join Nelly on the song. The hook of the song begins:

> I said it must be ya ass cause it ain't ya face/ I need a Tip Drill, I need a Tip Drill/

In the aftermath of the controversy social critics wanted to know why would Nelly at the height of his rap career release a video that insulted and degraded Black females, especially during a time when he was soliciting the support of the public to find a bone marrow donor for his sister who was diagnosed with acute leukemia. No donor was found and she later died. The backlash from the controversy, coupled with her death, led him to take a brief hiatus from the public eye.

Participants in the control group were asked to watch then-feminist rap artist Queen Latifah's 1989 video, *Ladies First*. The video features Queen Latifah along with rap artist Monie Love. It begins with photographs of Black female abolitionists, Harriet Tubman and Sojourner Truth, each influential in fighting against gender inequality. They both worked tirelessly in the struggle to free slaves and gain freedom and equal rights. The lyrics discuss women's empowerment and stress the importance of women being accepted as equals in the rap music industry. During her most passionate verse, Queen Latifah raps:

> Who said the ladies couldn't make it, you must be blind/ If you don't believe, well here, listen to this rhyme/ Ladies first, there's no time to rehearse/ I'm divine and my mind expands throughout the universe/

Participants viewed the video and were provided with a copy of the lyrics for the entire song. Afterward, they were asked to perform the survey.

Survey Results

Rap music was most popular among male college students. One male participant, Junior, 22, replied on the survey, "I love rap music. I can appreciate all kinds of rap [music]." Forty-three percent of those in the experimental group responded they listen to rap music *very frequently*. Levels of agreement varied in other categories, *frequent* (15 percent), *sometimes* (19 percent), *rarely* (23 percent), and *never* (0 percent). Male participants made up the majority of the *very frequent* (62 percent) category. On the other hand, females represented the bulk of the *rarely* (60 percent) category. Similar findings were in the control group. Forty-nine percent responded they listen to rap music *very frequently*, *frequent* (21 percent), *sometimes* (16 percent), *rarely* (7 percent), and *never* (7 percent). According to one female participant in the experimental group, Sophomore, 19, "I don't like rap music. I only listen to it if I am in the club. I just like the beat." Her response was consistent that of most female participants.

When asked in the experimental group, "What do you pay attention to most when listening to rap music?" 87 percent of females said they were solely fans of the *instrumental beat*. Males paid attention to all facets of rap songs in the experimental group, the *instrumental beat* (25 percent), *lyrical content* (43 percent), and *both equally* (32 percent). In the control group, 91 percent of females responded they only listen to the *instrumental beat*. Males listened to both elements, *lyrical content* (46 percent) and *both equally* (35 percent).

General attitudes toward rap music were split. Overall, 57 percent of participants in the experimental group believed rap music was *positive*, whereas 36 percent responded it was *negative*. Only seven percent were *neutral*. There was a significant gender difference when participants were asked how they would classify their attitudes toward rap music. Eighty-seven percent of males had a positive attitude toward rap music, whereas 93 percent of females had a negative attitude. In the control group, 94 percent of males had a positive attitude toward rap music and a lower percentage of females (81 percent) possessed a negative attitude. When asked, "Do you believe that rap songs are more offensive to males or females or both?" unequivocally all participants in both groups believed it was solely offensive to females. One female participant in the control group, Senior, 23, replied in the survey, "Rap music has become the worst musical art form. It never has anything positive to say about or to women." Ironically, males in the experimental group who reported they listened to rap music *very frequently* and paid attention to all facets had a positive attitude toward rap songs but agreed it is most offensive to females.

When asked, "Which misogynistic theme do you find most offensive in rap music?" both males and females (49 percent) in the experimental group agreed that the theme of *sexual assault and rape* was most offensive. The *legitimation of physical violence against females* (24 percent), *derogatory name-calling* (16 percent), and *prostitution and pimping* (11 percent) followed. One female participant in this group, Freshman, 19, believed that rap music is responsible for the sexually aggressive behavior of Black males. She replied in the survey when asked about the current state of rap music, "The songs tell boys to do stupid stuff. In high school I had a boy try to pull me into the bathroom and have sex with me. When I said 'no' he repeated some rap lyric from Drake [and Trey Songz], 'I invented sex.' You are 17 but you invented sex, yeah right." Fifty-three percent of females in the experimental group found the misogynistic theme of *sexual assault and rape* most offensive compared to 47 percent of males. The *legitimation of physical violence against females* ranked second among both females (27 percent) and males (23 percent). The misogynistic theme of *derogatory name-calling* ranked lower. Twenty-one percent of males and 7 percent of females reported this misogynistic theme to be offensive. In comparison, those in the control group found that *legitimation of physical violence against females* ranked first followed by *derogatory name-calling, sexual assault and rape,* and *prostitution and pimping.*

The majority of participants in the experimental group *strongly agreed* (65 percent) that rap music provokes disrespectful attitudes toward females. Gender differences showed that a greater percentage of females (70 percent) took this position than males (62 percent). According to one male participant in this group, Junior, 21, "Rap music often gets a bad rap for showing women in a negative light. I think women are willing to do videos, be half dressed and let guys slap their butt and throw money on them. They could always refuse to be in the videos." Fifty-six percent of those in the control group also *strongly agreed* and 21 percent *somewhat agreed* that rap music provokes disrespectful attitudes toward females. When participants in the experimental group were asked, "Do you believe that rap music promotes aggressive and violent behavior toward females?" the majority (58 percent) *strongly agreed*. Twenty percent *somewhat agreed*. Fifteen percent *somewhat disagreed* and 5 percent *strongly disagreed*; however those were all males. By gender, 90 percent of females *strongly agreed*. In contrast, 40 percent of males *strongly agreed* and 26 percent *somewhat agreed*. In comparison, the control group observed a lower percentage of those that believed rap music promotes aggressive and violent behavior toward females. Gender differences show that 35 percent of males *strongly disagreed*, while 71 percent of females *strongly agreed*.

To further explore the attitudes of participants regarding the misogynistic message of sexual assault and rape, participants in both groups were asked, "Do you believe that rap music encourages the sexual assault and rape of females?" Sixty-three percent of participants in the experimental group *strongly agreed* and 23 percent *somewhat agreed*. Ten percent *strongly disagreed*. Again, those were all males. Ninety-seven percent of females *strongly agreed*. One female in this group, Junior, 20, replied on the survey, "Rap music has too much influence on men and little boys. Besides calling women bitches and hoes, it [also] tells them to slap chicks, take the cookie and leave us if we don't act right. I'm trying to get my little brother to stop listening to this garbage. The song played today disgusts me. I had never heard it before." Forty-three percent of males *strongly agreed* and 34 percent *somewhat agreed* that rap music encourages the sexual assault and rape of females. One male participant in this group, Sophomore, 19, stated, "The current state of rap music sucks because all they talk about is money and hoes. If you have money, you can have all the hoes you want. I don't listen to mainstream rap like JayZ, [Young] Jeezy and Lil Wayne. They degrade women. I have a mother and two sisters at home. God forbid someone disrespects them by calling them bitches and hoes or talking about raping them."

In the control group, 61 percent of participants *strongly agreed*. The bulk were female, 77 percent, who believed that rap music encourages the sexual assault and rape of females. One female, Senior, 21, argued, "We need more images like this [*Ladies First* video] in rap music. It would help to stop dudes that believe they can handle us any kind of way. I was excited to see that type of video. Dudes see the booty videos and think they are the rappers. A lot of dudes have no respect for females anymore. I've had several dudes try to take it from me."

When asked, "Do you believe that rap music shapes male listener's attitudes toward sexually assaulting and raping females?" 39 percent of participants in the experimental group *strongly agreed*. Levels of agreement varied among participants, *somewhat agreed* (14 percent), *neutral* (6 percent), *somewhat disagree* (16 percent), and *strongly disagree* (25 percent). Males represented all of the *somewhat disagree* and *strongly disagree* categories. Eighty-seven percent of females *strongly agreed*, whereas, 40 percent of males *strongly disagreed* that rap music shapes male listeners' attitudes toward sexually assaulting and raping females. According to one male, Junior, 21, in an attempt to decipher the influence of rap lyrics, "Rap music is an expression. It expresses the good and bad. We let the bad overshadow the good. Personally, I'm not going to talk negative to women or try to have sex with everyone I see. I know guys that do that." A similar breakup was found in the control group. Forty-four percent *strongly agree*, *somewhat agreed* (10 percent), *neutral* (5 percent), *somewhat disagree* (10 percent), and *strongly disagree* (31 percent). Males were most represented in the category of *strongly disagree* (73 percent) and females in the category of *strongly agree* (74 percent). Males in both groups disagreed that rap music shapes their attitudes toward sexually assaulting and raping females. In contrast, females agreed that rap music has the ability to shape male listeners' attitudes. One female, Freshman, 19, in the experimental group expressed, "I don't like rap music. All they rap about is sex. I had a guy randomly text me and ask for "*Birthday Sex*." You know he heard the song by [R&B artist] Jeremih. When they hear these songs they think they can do and say what the rappers do and say."

When asked, "Do you believe that rap artists should be more accountable for their lyrical content?" 93 percent of those in the experimental group *strongly agreed*. The lack of variation of this question continues a perplexing trend considering that 87 percent of males had a positive attitude toward rap music despite the bulk agreeing that it disrespected females.

The one open-ended question in the survey, "What are your thoughts on the current state of rap music?" helps to explain Black males' love and support for rap music regardless of the misogynistic messages that degrade Black females. When participants were asked this question, the majority of Black males had positive feedback. According to one male, Senior, 24:

> Rap music is in good hands. I'm a fan of mainstream rap [music] and underground rap [music]. I do believe that rappers should be more accountable for their lyrical content but honestly it is a part of the culture. They've been saying "nigger," "bitch," and "ho[e]" in songs long before I was born. That won't stop. I do wish there would be more songs that rap about being a successful Black man. That would bring more balance to rap music.

Other responses from Black males about the current state of rap music from both groups were:

> *Freshman, 18*: The current state is great. I'm a rapper myself. I make music that the women like to listen to. It's all about pleasing them. And they like the vulgar stuff. They like the booty shaking music. You should see how they dance to it. They love it.

Sophomore, 20: Rappers are just keeping it real in their songs. I don't like watered down rap music. Nobody wants to hear that. I don't agree with DMX in his song but it is, what it is.

Sophomore, 20: Rap music has two big stars, Lil Wayne and JayZ. [Lil] Wayne is garage. All he raps about is BS. Jay is cool, but his music is outdated. None of their lyrics uplift Black people but I still like listening to it. I'm just a fan of rap music.

Junior, 21: I love rap music. I don't like some of the messages, but I do love the music.

Senior, 22: Rap music is in a flux. There are a bunch of rappers who are just gimmicks. They rap about whatever is happening at the time. I'll be honest, I still listen because that's all I know. I grow up on rap [music]. I don't like R&B, country and rock and roll. So I listen to rap [music]. I do believe these dudes should watch what they rap about. Some of it is over the top.

The baseline survey administered to college students to record their attitudes about misogynistic messages in rap music identifies several important points (see tables 2.2 and 2.3). First, exposure to the misogynistic elements had a greater influence on the experimental group according to the higher scores on responses. Second, the majority of males had a positive attitude toward rap music despite agreeing that it disrespected females and rap artists should be more accountable for their lyrical content. Third, males in both groups disagreed that rap music shapes their attitudes toward sexually assaulting and raping females. In contrast, females agreed that rap music has the ability to shape male listeners' attitudes. Some described incidents in which they believed rap music had an influence on their response to the open-ended question. Responses to the open-ended question exposed a line of discourse to address whether Black males understand the cognitive priming ability of rap music, specifically songs that contain the misogynistic message of sexual assault and rape. Previous studies have found that lyrics and images in gangsta rap music and videos can cognitively prime listeners (Hansen 1995; Rudman and Lee 2002). Repetitive exposure to misogynistic messages that promote sexual aggression

Table 2.2 Summary of Baseline Survey, Experimental Group

	Strongly agree (5)	Somewhat agree (4)	Neutral (3)	Somewhat disagree (2)	Strongly disagree (1)	Response average
Do you believe that rap music provokes disrespectful attitudes toward females?	65% (54)	16% (13)	6% (5)	10% (8)	3% (3)	4.29
Do you believe that rap music promotes aggressive and violent behavior toward females?	58% (48)	20% (17)	2% (2)	15% (12)	5% (4)	4.12
Do you believe that rap music encourages the sexual assault and rape of females?	63% (52)	23% (19)	2% (2)	2% (2)	10% (8)	4.27
Do you believe that rap music shapes male listeners' attitudes toward sexually assaulting and raping females?	39% (32)	14% (12)	6% (5)	16% (13)	25% (21)	3.25
Do you believe that rap artists should be more accountable for their lyrical content?	93% (77)	5% (4)	2% (2)	0% (0)	0% (0)	4.86

Total = 83

Table 2.3 Summary of Baseline Survey, Control Group

	Strongly agree (5)	Somewhat agree (4)	Neutral (3)	Somewhat disagree (2)	Strongly disagree (1)	Response average
Do you believe that rap music provokes disrespectful attitudes toward females?	56% (34)	21% (13)	10% (6)	8% (5)	5% (3)	4.15
Do you believe that rap music promotes aggressive and violent behavior toward females?	43% (26)	16% (10)	12% (7)	13% (8)	16% (10)	3.56
Do you believe that rap music encourages the sexual assault and rape of females?	61% (37)	15% (9)	5% (3)	3% (2)	16% (10)	4.00
Do you believe that rap music shapes male listener's attitudes toward sexually assaulting and raping females?	44% (27)	10% (6)	5% (3)	10% (6)	31% (19)	3.26
Do you believe that rap artists should be more accountable for their lyrical content?	95% (53)	5% (3)	0% (0)	0% (0)	0% (0)	4.95

Total = 61

could potentially compromise their social judgment and lead them to believe that such behavior is justified (Hall and Hirschman 1991).

Conclusion

This chapter has talked about the negative societal impact of rap music. The objective of this chapter was to open up a dialogue on whether rap lyrics that celebrate the objectification and sexual abuse of women influence the behavior of Black males. As a whole, it is difficult to deny that rap music does not encourage Black males to commit sexual violence against Black females. The last two decades has witnessed more songs containing the misogynistic message of sexual assault and rape. Is a "rape culture" manifesting in rap music? Or are artists being lyrically irresponsible? Rap artists have a duty to consciously educate and inform youth today. Excessive violent and misogynistic messages must be curtailed, by the discretion of the artist, in order to reduce the hypothesized effects of rap music leading to the acceptance of violence against women. Rap songs that contain misogynistic messages coupled with videos that exploit females carry a socially destructive message to the younger generation of Black males and females who may not be able to cognitively interpret the lyrics and images as mere entertainment.

The current state of rap music systematically supports the oppressive system it once defied. A number of rap artists do not project positive messages that uplift the Black community. Rap music has gone from Public Enemy's *Fight the Power*, which informed the Black community that "what we need is awareness/ we can't get careless," to Young Money's, *Every Girl*, which boasts "I wish I could fuck every girl in the world,"a message now embedded in the misogynistic culture of rap music. While hip-hop scholars have argued that rap music is simply a by-product of a misogynistic American culture, that excuse should no longer be tolerated. The art form is no longer being used primarily as an agent of cultural and social change, but it is a modern day minstrel show whereby Black male rap artists perform in indistinguishable Black face and appeal to the stereotypes and stigmas of White America to hopefully generate album sales. In the words of hip-hop icon Lauryn Hill, in her 1998 song *Superstar*, "Hip-hop, started out in the heart/ Now everybody's trying to chart...Music is suppose to inspire/ So, how come we ain't getting no higher?"

CHAPTER 3

Black-on-Black Murders: A Case Study of Chiraq, Killinois

In the rap song *Murder to Excellence*, artist Kayne West, a Chicago native, begins the chorus with the following lyrics, "The paper read, 'murder, black-on-black murder.'" The lyrical content in this song describes the malicious Black-on-Black murders that have consumed the city of Chicago for over a decade. He raps:

> It's a war going on outside we ain't safe from/ I feel the pain in my city wherever I go/ 314 soldiers died in Iraq/ 509 died in Chicago/

Each year national data from the Bureau of Justice Statistics (BJS) report that most crimes are intraracial. For example, in 2011 nationwide Black offenders killed 93 percent of Black victims. Hence, Black-on-Black murders are not a new phenomenon but the frequency in which they occur identifies a disturbing trend in the Black community. A trend that has reached epic proportions in the Black male subculture.

In the city of Chicago, at least one Black person is killed every day. The Chicago Police Department (CPD) has recorded an estimated total of 6,094 murders in the past decade (see table 3.1). From 2001 to 2003, the total number of murders each year was above 600. Despite decreasing patterns after 2003, it again climbed to over 500 murders in 2008 and 2012. In 2012 the city had 506 murders, increasing

Table 3.1   Total Murders in Chicago, 2001–2012

2001	667
2002	656
2003	601
2004	453
2005	451
2006	471
2007	448
2008	513
2009	459
2010	436
2011	433
2012	506
Total	**6,094**

Source: Chicago Police Department, 2001–2012 Murder Analysis Report.

the murder rate by more than 19 percent (433) than what was reported in 2011. The city reclaimed the title "Murder Capital of the World." While other major metropolitan cities have had higher murder rates based on total population, Chicago has consistently had the highest number of murders per year in the last decade. Cities like Washington, DC and New Orleans have seen a significant decrease in murders since the mid-part of the decade while Chicago's murder count has almost doubled and nearly tripled their total numbers of murders (see table 3.2). Compared to New York, which is three times the size of Chicago, the city of Chicago still had 92 more murders in 2012.

The vast majority of murders in the city are a result of Black-on-Black gun violence. A large proportion of these murders occur in Black communities on the South and West sides of the city where gang violence is a key contributing factor to the total deaths of Black males. According to the 2010 US Census, Blacks made up 32.9 percent of the city's population. In 2012, 69 percent of the victims of murder were Black males. At the halfway point from January to July, 201 of the 259 murder victims were Black, accounting for nearly 78 percent of murder victims. From 2003 to 2011, 75 percent of the victims of an estimated 4,265 murders were Black. In

Table 3.2 Metropolitan Cities with High Murder Totals, 2001–2012

Year	Washington, DC	New Orleans, LA	Detroit, MI	New York, NY
2001	232	213	395	649*
2002	264	258	402	587
2003	248	274	366	597
2004	198	264	385	570
2005	195	–	354	539
2006	169	162	418	596
2007	181	209	394	496
2008	186	179	306	523
2009	143	174	365	471
2010	132	175	310	536
2011	108	200	344	515
2012	88	193	411	414

Note: The table does not include the 2,823 homicides reported in the September 11, 2001, terrorist attack; FBI UCR 2005 does not have data for New Orleans, LA.

Source: Crime in the United States, Uniform Crime Reports, Federal Bureau of Investigation.

Table 3.3 Percentage of Murder Victims in Chicago, 2007–2011

Year	All male victims	Black victims only	All age group (17–25) victims
2007	87	75	40
2008	88	72	42
2009	88	76	43
2010	88	76	40
2011	90	75	45

Source: Chicago Police Department, 2007–2011 Murder Analysis Report

2011 alone, 75 percent of the 433 murder victims were Black (see table 3.3).[1] Just as daunting is that Blacks have been the offenders in a high percentage of these murders. According to the CPD Murder Analysis report, Blacks have been the offender and victim in over 76 percent of the total murders in the last decade (see table 3.4).[2] The bulk of these individuals are young Black males between the ages of 17 and 25.

One of the participants, Brad, Educator, 37, stated, "Chicago is a war zone. I'm saddened to see Black males killing each other. These young dudes don't care about life. They [are] killing each other over bullshit and nonsense. It makes

Table 3.4   Percentage of Murder Offenders in Chicago, 2007–2011

Year	All male offenders	Black offenders only	All age group (17–25) offenders
2007	90	72	44
2008	91	80	52
2009	93	74	53
2010	93	76	49
2011	88	71	53

Source: Chicago Police Department, 2007–2011 Murder Analysis Report.

me ashamed and afraid to be a Black man at the same time." Brad's comments were correct. The city of Chicago is much like a war zone. With such a high murder count the media in 2012 bestowed Chicago a new label, "Chiraq," indicating that the death toll is comparable to *Operation Iraqi Freedom.* This war started on March 20, 2003, and ended December 15, 2011, recording a total of 4,422 casualties. In that same time frame Chicago recorded just fewer than 4200 murders.[3] What underscores the comparison of Chicago murders with wars overseas is the fact that many of those being killed are innocent adult bystanders and children, the collateral damage of the dehumanization of Black human life in the city.

The national spotlight on the city's murders intensified after the killing of Hadiya Pendleton, a Black female high school honor student who attended President Obama's second-term inauguration ceremony. Pendleton was shot and killed by a stray bullet on January 29, 2013, at a park near her school on the South side, just one mile from Obama's Chicago home. She was talking with a male friend who was falsely mistaken as a gang member. After that incident the CPD assigned 200 more administrative officers to patrol as a preventable measure to fight against the murder epidemic.

Many Black Chicagoans had asked how could the city of Chicago, the home of President Obama, consistently have such a high number of Black murders each year? Why hadn't Obama provided substantive representation for Black Chicagoans in an attempt to alleviate Black-on-Black violence?

This issue further ignited an underlying criticism of Obama about his lack of substantive policies for Black Americans during his presidency.[4] He broke his silence in the latter part of 2012 during an interview with *MTV News*, in which he expressed the following regarding Chicago murders:

> I live on the South side of Chicago. Some of these murders are happening just a few blocks from where I live. I have friends whose family members have been killed.
>
> What I know is that gun violence is part of the issue. But part of the issue also is kids who feel so little hope and think their prospects for the future are so small that their attitude is, "I'm going to end up in jail or dead." And they will take all kinds of risks.[5]

Despite addressing the constant gun violence in Chicago, public clamor remained for Obama to assert his political authority. One of the Chicago natives in this study, Ron, Police Officer, 46, voiced strong concern about Obama and gun violence:

> Obama has dropped the ball on Chicago murders. I'm disappointed in the way he has handled the situation. Even as a state legislator and [U.S.] senator the deaths of Black males was not a priority for him. He never made gun control a top priority in either one of those political positions. Does he really care about the death of Black males? I'm disappointed that this is not a priority.

Although the state of Illinois already has some of the toughest gun control laws in the United States, gun violence has reached epidemic proportions. More than 2400 gun-related shootings were reported to the CPD in 2011. A total of 361 murders were committed with firearms (83 percent). Just a year earlier, handguns were banned until a 2010 US Supreme Court decision overturned the law.[6] The city has drawn criticism from proponents of gun control laws who wish to reinforce legislative oversight and introduce new legislation for tougher gun laws. Political pressure at all levels of government has led to the renewed discussion of gun control legislation in Illinois. Opponents of stricter gun control laws suggest that the state already has substantial legislation. They believe the failure to control gun violence is a dereliction of duty by Mayor Rahm Emanuel, former chief of staff for the Obama Administration, as well as by Police Superintendent Garry McCarthy in not implementing efficient policing strategies in high-violence neighborhoods. In a July 2013 press conference, Superintendent McCarthy, standing before more than 4,000 guns seized by Chicago police mostly during gang arrests just that year, expressed that stronger sentencing laws would also help to combat the gun violence:

> Too many guns on the streets coming in, not enough sentencing at the back end, results in more gun violence. We can do a lot of things in between, but until such time as the criminal justice system as a whole supports reducing gun violence we're going to be stuck in the same place.[7]

In the press conference, McCarthy also explained that most of the shooting victims were gang members (see table 3.5). However, due to poor marksmanship these gang-related shootings have taken the lives of many innocent bystanders. He proposed that a long-term solution would be to enforce mandatory minimum sentences for those in possession of a loaded, unlawfully owned handgun.

The public outcry from Chicago residents, coupled with national attention in the aftermath of the Sandy Hook

Table 3.5   Gun-Related Murders in Chicago, 2007–2011

Year	No. of murders by shooting	% of murders by shooting
2007	328	73
2008	412	80
2009	375	82
2010	351	81
2011	361	83
Total	1,827	80

Source: Chicago Police Department, 2007–2011 Murder Analysis Report.

Elementary school shooting in Newton, Connecticut, that claimed the lives of twenty children and six staff members, led to a fervent national gun control debate. President Obama made the following statement after the Sandy Hook tragedy: "We're going to have to come together and take meaningful action to prevent more tragedies like this, regardless of the politics."[8] This prompted Obama in January 2013 to sign 23 Executive Orders to address the issue of gun violence. Some of the more substantial Executive Orders signed proposed strengthening background checks, banning military-style assault weapons and high-capacity magazines, and making school zones safer.[9] He also called on Congress to pass more specific measures that include tougher penalties on those who legally buy and resell guns that eventually find their way on the underground market and in the hands of young Black males.

Despite attempts to introduce and pass proactive gun control laws at the state level, the majority of members in the Illinois General Assembly voted in July 2013 to adopt a "concealed to carry" gun law. Illinois was the last state in the country to pass such legislation. Opponents of this law identified it as counterproductive in the fight against gun violence claiming that it would further damage public safety. During the Fourth of July weekend days prior to its passage, the city of Chicago witnessed 74 people shot and 12 murdered.

Democratic governor Pat Quinn initially vetoed parts of the bill in its original form because it allowed citizens to carry two guns and possess guns in public places that served alcohol; however, a majority of both chambers of the Assembly voted to override his decision. The Senate (41–17) and House (77–31) voted overwhelmingly in favor of this measure; however, all Black legislators in both chambers voted against this bill.[10] During the legislative process, Black state senator Kimberly Lightford was concerned that various forms of the bills were "too loosely written" and "doesn't protect us at all."[11]

To offset the newly passed concealed to carry law, legislators and City Council members from Chicago soon followed with new preventive gun control laws. Black state senator

Kwame Raoul (D-Chicago) along with state representative Mike Zalewski (D-Riverside) sponsored an important gun-control measure that was signed into law in August by Governor Quinn. The new bill expanded background checks on all firearm purchases, including private gun sales whereby many believed is the medium through which guns flood the streets of Chicago.[12] Gun buyers must possess a firearm owners identification (FOID) card, which is only issued by the Illinois state police to applicants who pass a series of screening tests.[13] An important component of the new law was that it required gun owners to report lost or stolen weapons to the CPD within 72 hours. Additionally, Mayor Emanuel and his administration passed more strict gun-safety laws, one of which was a measure to protect students by increasing "penalties for serious weapon and gun-related offenses in 'student safety zones.'"[14]

In this chapter, I seek to add to our knowledge about the determinants that lead to the increasing number of Black-on-Black murders involving gun violence in the city of Chicago. While I have outlined the governmental and legislative strategies above to address the issue of gun violence, the central goal is to focus on the structural and cultural factors that continue to propel these Black-on-Black murders. We understand that this epidemic is multilayered and cannot be blamed on governmental action and guns alone. It is imperative that we identify why some Black males continue to pull the trigger and take the lives of other Black males.

Factors behind the continuance of Black-on-Black murders in Chicago have ranged from the social disorganization of the environment, lack of education, high Black unemployment, generational poverty, absentee fathers, territorial battles between gangs, drug wars, to the devaluing of Black human life. As we attempt to contribute to the understanding of this impasse that has persisted for decades, it is important to revisit several of these structural and cultural forces that underline the everyday realities of Black males in "Chiraq, Killinois."

The Uneducated Black Male

There is a sizeable gap in educational success among Black males and other demographics in Chicago Public Schools (CPS). In 2010 they had the highest dropout rate of any other demographic in CPS. One in eight Black males dropped out of school. Only 44 percent achieved a high school diploma.[15] In that same year, President Obama proposed a new educational program titled *Race to the Top*, which gave $900 million in federal grants to low-performing schools to address the school dropout crisis across the country and boost the quality of education for all Americans. To qualify for funding, school districts would need to agree to a list of criteria that included the closure of failing schools nationwide.[16] Obama stressed the importance of education in his speech before the US Chamber of Commerce on March 1, 2010:

> And we know that the success of every American will be tied more closely than ever before to the level of education that they achieve. The jobs will go to the people with the knowledge and the skills to do them—it's that simple. In this kind of knowledge economy, giving up on your education and dropping out of school means not only giving up on your future, but it's also giving up on your family's future and giving up on your country's future.
>
> Graduating from high school is an economic imperative. That might be the best reason to get a diploma, but it's not the only reason to get a high school diploma...high school dropouts are more likely to be teen parents, more likely to commit crime, more likely to rely on public assistance, more likely to lead shattered lives.[17]

The quality of public education in Chicago has long been under question and subject to intense scrutiny. The city has the third largest school district in the United States, serving nearly half a million students, 90 percent of whom are students of color and 84 percent are from low-income families (Lipman 2002, 380). In the past decade, Chicago has closed more than 80 underperforming and underutilized schools.[18] CPS had indicated the closures were a way of improving the quality of low-performing schools. In May 2013, the Chicago Board of Education approved the closure of 50 public schools. CPS explained the recent closures were an effort to restructure and reallocate funding needed to improve current schools and open charter schools. Greg, a Chicago native, Educator, 47, expressed his disgust about the quality of public schools, "I'm from Chicago. They are closing schools left and right. We keep saying education and providing economic opportunities will reduce the murder rate, but we close the school. Those students do not attend schools in other neighborhoods because they fear gang violence. In turn, they drop out."

To Greg's point, Mayor Emanuel, Police Superintendent McCarthy, and Public Schools CEO Barbara Byrd-Bennett have created and implemented a program titled *Safe Passage*, which is intended to offer students a safe route to and from school to ensure their safety. In 2012 there were more than 600 safe passage workers to serve CPS; however, the city still saw its greatest number of murders in recent years (506).[19]

The shutdown of 50 CPS campuses represented the largest closure of public schools at one time in recent years. Opponents feared obvious racial repercussions, understanding it would disproportionately affect low-income Black students. The racial implications of school closings have always been a subject of scholarly reviews. Thomas S. Martin (1972, 668) in his article about inequality in Black school closings suggests that the standards used for school closings should put emphasis on its discriminating effect, rather than its intended purpose.

There continues to be concern relative to potential worsening of the academic performance of Black male students who, in general, already show remarkably higher dropout rates and lower graduation rates compared with their White counterparts. Black male high school students in CPS have lagged behind Whites and Hispanics (see table 3.6). Data gathered from CPS for 2007 to 2012 show that Black males fell behind considerably in their pace to graduate high school

Table 3.6 Percentage of Male Freshman Students On-Track Rate in Chicago Public Schools (CPS), by Race/Ethnicity, 2007–2012

Race/Ethnicity	2007	2008	2009	2010	2011	2012
Black	43.6	47.2	52.8	58	61.4	63
White	65.4	67.6	71.3	76.5	78.9	81
Hispanic	52.6	52.5	57	62.5	69	69.9

Note: On-track rate represents rating of first-time CPS freshman students. Per CPS measure, students are on-track if at the end of their freshman year they earned at least five course credits and failed no more than one semester course in a core subject (English, Math, Social Science, or Science).

Source: Chicago Public Schools (CPS), Research Evaluation Accountability (REA) 2007–2012.

in four years. From the onset of their enrollment, they display poorer academic performance compared to other students. Per CPS reports, the on-track indicator shows that high school freshmen designated as on-track are three and a half times more likely to graduate from high school in four years than students who are off-track.

The dropout rate among Black male high school students was significantly higher than Whites and Hispanics. Table 3.7 shows that more than half of Black males in CPS have dropped out of high school from 2007 to 2012. The significant dropout rates coincide with lower graduation rates for Black males. Table 3.8 illustrates that while the graduate rate for Black males has increased in CPS, it has not exceeded 50 percent. The high school graduation gap between Black and White males in CPS is widening. In 2012 there was a 15.1 percent gap. The graduate rate for Black males was only 44.5 percent compared to 59.6 percent for White males. Huge pools of Black males in CPS drop out of high school and do not receive their diploma.

Greg offered another thought on the low graduation rate of Black males in CPS. He stated, "If the Mayor and CPS really wanted to address youth violence, they would make sure that schools stayed open. Their mission should be to improve current schools rather than closing them. It has been my experience that uneducated, poor kids are eventually going to commit crimes and kill if need be."

Table 3.7 Dropout % among Male High School Students in Chicago Public Schools (CPS), by Race/Ethnicity, 2007–2012

Race/Ethnicity	2007	2008	2009	2010	2011	2012
Black	55	53.8	54.5	54.1	51.3	50.9
White	41.1	41.3	40.2	38.6	34.3	32.4
Hispanic	47	47.9	46.9	43.8	39.7	35.5

Note: Rates are based on 5-year cohort dropout rates. For example, 2007 rate tracks ninth grade students who started in CPS in 2002–03 school year and dropped out of CPS by August 2006–07 school year (CPS, REA 2008).

Source: Chicago Public Schools (CPS), Research Evaluation Accountability (REA) 2007–2012.

Table 3.8 Graduation % among Male High School Students in Chicago Public Schools (CPS), by Race/Ethnicity, 2007–2012

Race/Ethnicity	2007	2008	2009	2010	2011	2012
Black	40.3	41.4	41.3	41.6	44.2	44.5
White	56.4	56.7	57.3	59.1	62.9	65.5
Hispanic	48.9	48.2	48.9	52.3	56.2	59.6

Note: Rates are based on 5-year cohort dropout rates. For example, 2007 rate tracks ninth grade students who started in CPS in 2002–03 school year and dropped out of CPS by August 2006–07 school year (CPS, REA 2008).

Source: Chicago Public Schools (CPS), Research Evaluation Accountability (REA) 2007–2012.

No Work for Black Males

In 2011, the city of Chicago had one of the highest Black unemployment rates in the nation at 19.1 percent. Chicago ranked third among major metropolitan cities.[20] Edward, Entrepreneur, 32, when asked why Black males are killing each other stated, "There are no jobs for them. As the old adage states, 'An idle mind is the devil's workshop.'" Available employment opportunities for Black males in Chicago are scarce. This emerges as a contributing factor that influences Black-on-Black murders. As William J. Wilson describes in his 1996 book, *When Work Disappears*, the impact of joblessness is significant in the Black community. The majority of uneducated Black males are limited to low-skilled manual work. When these job opportunities are not available, levels of poverty increase and the rate of crime goes up in the Black community. Wilson argues that many of today's problems in the inner-city are a microcosm of the disappearance of work.

Herb Boyd (2007, 2) in his study of the plight of Black males indicates, "One in four black men has not worked for at least a year, twice the proportion of male non-Hispanic whites or Latinos." In reference to the inability to find employment, Thomas, Contractor, 31 stated, "I went without work for almost two years. I looked for construction jobs, warehousing jobs, landscaping jobs, almost any job I could find. I have years of work experience and folks wouldn't even hire me for an entry level job." His story was similar to other Black males interviewed. Wilson, in *When Work Disappears*, found that a majority of employers, Black and White, in the greater Chicago area expressed negative views about uneducated Black males from the inner-city and were reluctant to provide them with entry-level jobs.

Most participants in this study believed that many Black males are reluctant to work certain jobs. They possess a sense of entitlement even without having a high school diploma or college degree. Some Black males do not "dress to impress" nor present themselves in a "professional manner," which eliminates them from job consideration during the interview process. Others do not have the "technological skills" needed to be able to compete in the current global workforce, and experience not racial discrimination, but technological discrimination. Thus they are relegated to blue-collar employment. On the other hand, there were some who expressed similar sentiments as the findings from Wilson whereby employers often discriminated in the hiring of Black males from certain areas. Samuel, Graduate Student, 29, explained, "When you put on a resume you live in the projects or hood, the chances of getting an interview or the job are limited." In a qualitative study that examined joblessness of Black males aged 16–30 from the West side of Chicago, Laseter (1997) concluded that a geographic shift of jobs from the inner-city to suburbs coupled with hiring discrimination each play major roles in joblessness. Only 8.7 percent of Black teens aged 16–19 were employed in Chicago compared to 21 percent for Whites in a study by researchers at Northeastern University.[21] The researchers concluded that gainful employment of teens deters their involvement in deviant activities.

According to the US Census Bureau's 2011 American Community Survey, Chicago also had the third highest rate of those living below half of the poverty line among major cities. Twenty-one percent of Chicagoans lived in poverty compared to 13.1 percent for the state. This level of extreme poverty makes it difficult for those attempting to gain employment that would alleviate their current economic condition. Alfred, Minister, 51, relayed this thought about Black male unemployment and poverty: "I try to help young men find employment, but it is hard without a high school diploma. Many of these young men are so impoverished and down on their luck I know that if they do not find employment, they'll seek a life of crime. They can barely make ends meet. In many cases, they are the primary providers in the household because there is no father."

Absentee Fathers

The Black community has the highest proportion of children living in households without their biological father (Kreider and Ellis 2011). Quincy, Student, 20, said while discussing the effect of being reared in a single-parent household, "I have never met my father. I had to learn to be a man on my own. My mother depended on me to work. I almost quit school in the 10th grade to help bring money into the house." Scholars have attributed family instability to high rates of school dropout, which disrupts the lives of many Black youth and trails as a major contributing factor to consequent adult unemployment or underemployment (Davis, Ajzen, Saunders, and Williams 2002; Laseter 1997; Sander 1985). Specifically, young Black males are less likely to see

Table 3.9 Type of Household Percentage of Chicago Teenagers 15–19 Years Old, by Race/Ethnicity, 2007–2011

Type of Household	Black	White	Hispanic
In married-couple family household	22.3	64.5	60.3
In male householder, no wife present, family household	7.6	6.1	11.2
In female householder, no husband present, family household	68.5	21.4	27.0
In non-family household	1.6	8	1.5
Total	100	100	100

Source: US Census Bureau, 2007–2011 American Community Survey (ACS).

models of male employment in the household, which has an adverse effect on them.

William Sander (1985), in his study of the link between single-parent households and economic change in Chicago in 1970 through 1980, found that over a decade the rate of single-parent households had increased, which eliminated a source of income and led to the inability of the mother to provide her children with a quality education. Table 3.9 shows that 68.5 percent of Black teens aged 15–19 in Chicago live in single-parent households headed by females compared to only 27 percent for Hispanic and 21 percent for Whites highlighting this glaring problem. Gill, Entrepreneur, 49, argued:

> When the father is not in the home, it thrusts these young males to become men. It's hard for the mother not to put certain pressures on him to help financially or babysit younger siblings. He is expected to handle those responsibilities and keep his grades up in school. That is tough. I know, because that young man was me at one time. The mother has to be mindful, that is her son not her husband.

A constant theme that materialized while discussing the education and employment of Black males was that many believed they would have achieved greater academic and career success if their fathers had been present in their lives. According to Lincoln, Cashier, 42:

> I often reflect on my life and dream what it would be like if I had a father.
>
> Maybe I would have graduated from college. Maybe I would have a better paying job. I know not having a father is no excuse. But I wanted a father in my life. My friends had fathers. I spent a lot time in my teen years and early 20s in and out of jail, getting in trouble. I may not have done that if I had a father. Things may have been different.

In a 2013 graduation speech before a predominantly Black male audience at the Morehouse College[22] in Atlanta, Georgia, President Obama explained how he broke the father-less cycle and chose not to be like his father who abandoned him in his childhood.

> I was raised by a heroic single mom, wonderful grandparents—made incredible sacrifices for me. And I know there are moms and grandparents here today who did the same thing for all of you. But I sure wish I had had a father who was not only present, but involved.
>
> Didn't know my dad. And so my whole life, I've tried to be for Michelle and my girls what my father was not for my mother and me. I want to break that cycle where a father is not at home, where a father is not helping to raise that son or daughter. I want to be a better father, a better husband, a better man.[23]

There were those in the Black community that felt Obama's message was condescending and demeaning, which called for Black male accountability and responsibility as a whole. He asked Black males to "transform the way we think about manhood" and avoid "excuses." Some saw Obama chastising Black males and acting as a surrogate father with his message. The majority of participants in this study agreed that the need for a father or father figure is important in honing the behaviors of Black males. Rena, Educator, 52, stated, "If there were more fathers in the home, there would be less Black males killing each other. I really believe that."

Gang Violence

Most violence crimes and Black-on-Black murders in Chicago are in neighborhoods on the South and West side of the city where street gangs fight over turf, sell drugs, and there are a large number of stolen and unregistered guns. The main gangs are the Gangster Disciples, Vice Lords, Black P. Stones, Latin Kings, and Black Disciples. A 2012 CPD gang audit found that there are more than 600 gang factions in the city of Chicago. As a result, the CPD makes an absorbent number of arrests each year of gang members. In 2012 over 40,000 identified gang members were arrested. According to table 3.10, more than 225,000 were arrested from 2007 to 2012. Despite arrest and incarceration, new members surface and become a part of the numerous gangs.

In 2011, there were 433 murders in the city. According to table 3.11, 27 percent of those murders were gang motivated according to the CPD report. Eighty-three percent (361) of the murders were committed with a firearm. Ted, Store Manager, 33, indicated, "These young dudes develop cliques and think they are bad. They are almost like gangs. But, look at the real gangs, like in Chicago that operate as corporate conglomerates. Some probably pay the police to look the other way. They battle over territory, sell drugs and act as a family. The family component is what attracts new members."

For the hopeless and helpless Black male youth who grow up lacking parental guidance and control in single-parent

Table 3.10   Gang Arrests in Chicago, 2007–2012

Year	Arrests made where offender was identified as a gang member
2007	41,293
2008	37,433
2009	36,958
2010	35,588
2011	33,090
2012	40,831
Total	225,193

Source: Chicago Police Department, 2007–2012 Murder Analysis Report.

Table 3.11 Percentage of Murders Motivated by Gangs and Drugs, 2007–2011

Year	Street gang altercations	% of murders (street gang altercations motive)	Gangland narcotics	% of murders (gangland narcotics motive)
2007	115	26%	38	8%
2008	185	36%	23	4%
2009	125	27%	22	5%
2010	117	27%	27	6%
2011	118	27%	26	6%
Total	660	29%	136	6%

Source: Chicago Police Department, 2007–2011 Murder Analysis Report.

households, gang membership represents a sense of family, and the deviant acts associated with it are a part of the gang culture. Cureton (2009) explains in his article how gangs have been a socialization agent for Black males:

> The inner city's street history is clear. The street gang (not the family or the church) is the most important social network organization for urban youth.
>
> Even though gang involvement has proven to be the surest way to end up a felon, convict, or dead, a significant number of marginalized Black youth continue to gravitate toward gansterism, whereas older males are finding it difficult to withdraw from the gangster lifestyle. (348)

Gangs have served as Black males' bonding agent in some subcultures. Research has found that joining a gang fosters strong, genuine alliances but, on the other hand, has the potential to cultivate intraracial mistrust and fuel gang feuds lasting for decades (Cureton 2009, 354). In their analysis of street gang disputes in Chicago between 1959 and 1962, Hughes and Short Jr. (2005, 43) found that retaliation was the common cause of gang altercations during this time period. This finding is germane to the current state of affairs in Chicago, given most Black-on-Black murders occur due to gang retaliation.

The dynamics of the gang conflict appear to have worsened as gang-related murders continue to increase each year. Territory disputes have become more intense as the demand for drugs has increased, specifically the highly profitable heroin market. Young Black males involved in gangs and drugs do what it takes to protect their turf and maintain their source of living, even if it means killing innocent people as collateral damage. From September 2006 to June 2007, at least 30 students in CPS were killed by shooting, stabbing, and strangling (Horton 2009; Klein 2008). Black male gang members take incalculable risks to be a part of their subcultures. Inevitably this leads to them devaluing the lives of others and killing other Black males.

Menace to Society

As stated above, Obama in his 2012 *MTV News* interview said that young Black males in Chicago have adopted the belief "I'm going to end up in jail or dead." Working from this hopeless philosophy deeply rooted in some Black urban cultures, many of them take on a "Menace II Society" attitude. In the 1993 film *Menace II Society*, one of the characters, Kevin "O-Dog" Anderson played by Larenz Tate, spawned an attitude that was adopted by a generation of Black males that has trickled down. As Leon, Carpenter, 37, explained, "I'm scared of these young niggas, they don't give a fuck. They don't care about life. You even look at them wrong and it may lead to gun play."

The film *Menace II Society* highlights the troubles of Black urban culture and shows how Black males devalue life, which leads to senseless murders. The main character, Caine played by Tyrin Turner, is a recent high school graduate who only went to school "half of the time" and was a low-level drug dealer. His father, a convicted felon, was killed in a drug deal and mother, a heroin addict, died from an overdose. He lives with his grandparents who try to instill strong morals and values amid living in challenging social and economic conditions. Caine is cast in the film as a Black male dealt a bad hand by life, and his actions represent a deliberate attempt to survive in the deprived environment in which he was born.

Caine's best friend, O-Dog, is cast as the polar opposite. He is described by Caine in the film as "the craziest nigga alive. America's nightmare, young, black, and didn't give a fuck." The film shows that O-Dog has no daily ambition beyond selling drugs, stealing cars, drinking beer, smoking weed, watching TV, and kickin' it with the fellas. In his world, there is no life beyond the confines of his environment, no models of success, and living to see another day is a major accomplishment. Years since the release of the film, O-Dog has become the life inspiration for many young Black males. The film is a Black urban classic. Black males spanning different generations still watch it repeatedly. The characters are larger than life. The mentality and lifestyle of many Black males from urban environments mirror that of O-Dog. Displeased with the detached nature of young Black males, Nathan, Entrepreneur, 31 offered this critique, "When you see these lil dudes coming your way, you need to go the other way. They will kill you, no questions asked. They killin' in the Chi [Chicago], N.O. [New Orleans], all over. I keep my gun loaded with one in the chamber." In a similar tone, Alexander, Lawyer, 29, made an important point regarding Black male influence in Chicago by stating, "Black males in Chicago should aspire to be like Obama. Instead, they want to be like [rap artist] Chief Keef. His dude boasts about toting guns and killing other Black males. The culture is not safe for young Black males."

The offenders (and victims) of Black-on-Black murders represent the "Typical Offender." They are Black, ages 17–25, from poor, urban communities. Projected characteristics are consistent with those found in Jeffrey Reiman and

Paul Leighton's famous book *The Rich Get Richer and the Poor Get Prison* (2013, 67–72) about the typical suspect in a serious crime. This image is what the authors call the "typical offender." These individuals are deemed to be the real dangers to society. Another participant, Randall, Student, 19, offered this critique of Black-on-Black murders: "These dudes smoke too much weed and listen to stupid rap music. Their mentality is all messed up. They kill each other and don't care. They don't love themselves so they kill others that look like them. And the fucked up part is that they don't tell who is doing the killing."

The pathology of their respective environment, coupled with structural and cultural factors, has led many Black males to make costly decisions, which lead to taking another Black male's life. *Menace II Society* gives examples of how some Black males act when engaged in confrontations with other Black males. They become actors in homicidal behavior, playing out violent scenes that have deadly consequences.

A scene of great significance occurs in the film after Caine's cousin is shot to death in a car robbery. Caine is also shot and spends several days in the hospital. After returning home, O-Dog comes to visit him. When the two attempt to leave, Caine's grandfather pleads with them to stop the violence. "Boys, the Lord didn't put you here to be shooting and killing each other," he says. After their conversation, Caine and O-Dog leave the house and upon exiting, the grandfather comes to door and asks, "Caine, do you care whether you live or die?" Caine's responds, "I don't know." At the end of the movie, Caine's fate was sealed. Ronnie, played by Jada Pickett, encourages Caine to leave his criminal life behind and move to Atlanta. Halfheartedly he agrees, but before he leaves a man he got into a physical confrontation with earlier murders Caine. The film then goes into a reflective mode during the shooting scene where Caine remembers, "My Grandpa asked me one time if I care whether I live or die. Yeah, I do. Now it's too late."

CONCLUSION

This chapter addressed Black-on-Black murders in the city of Chicago. Violence is rooted in the Black urban culture. A complex web of structural and cultural forces helps to explain this epidemic. According to hooks (2004, 131), "Black males today live in a world that pays them the most attention when they are violently acting out." Black males in Chicago are under an intense national spotlight. The blame game of who or what is most responsible for the continual Black-on-Black murders begs a question of accountability. Should there be an equal division of blame? The state of Illinois has some of the stiffest gun control laws in the country. The governor actively supports legislation that makes access of guns more stringent. Black state legislators have introduced and passed substantive gun control legislation in an attempt to offset the murder total in the city. The mayor and city council have passed policies to address gun violence. The CPD has implemented community-policing strategies in gang-concentrated areas.

What remains to be blamed is a failing educational system for poor Black males who come from single-parent households, join gangs, and eventually drop out of school. Either they work minimum-wage jobs, cannot find a job, or enter the drug trade. This contributes to the negative perception of Black males as criminals, low-skilled, and uneducated. However, one factor is most troubling—the lack of individual accountability of young Black males. They must be more accountable for their own actions. The idea of being a "menace to society," "thug," or "real nigga" is flattering in some Black male subcultures, but is gravely disingenuous to the plight, triumph, and preservation of Black male life.

Clearly, the onus lies solely on Black males to make responsible decisions with gun usage. If they desire to own guns, appropriate steps must be taken to obtain these legally and practice socially responsible behavior. The Darwinistic behavior of Black males in Chicago has to stop. The structural and cultural factors listed above do have a profound effect on their thinking and subsequent actions. But personal responsibility has to be employed to decrease the high number of Black-on-Black murders in the city year after year. Without question, it will take a community to act as change agents, offer a variety of solutions, and implement resources as appropriately needed.

CHAPTER 4

Living in the Obama Era

On November 6, 2012, President Obama handily beat his opponent, former Republican Massachusetts governor Mitt Romney, to win a second term in office. Obama beat Romney by capturing 51 to 49 percent of the popular vote and 332–206 Electoral College votes. In his victory speech, Obama conveyed that "despite all of our differences" we want future generations of children to grow up in an American society that is "respected and admired around the world." He described wanting to help foster an American societal climate that encourages children to dream beyond their current conditions. To even include "the young [Black] boy on the South Side of Chicago who sees a life beyond the nearest street corner." Obama stressed, "that's the future we hope for. That's the vision we share. That's where we need to go—Forward."[1]

The question of Obama's intent for the economic, social, and political advancement of Black Americans in general has been under scrutiny since he was elected to office in 2008. Critics question whether Obama could offer more than symbolic representation for the Black community. In both the 2008 and 2012 presidential elections Blacks showed tremendous loyalty in their vote support. But has Obama in return shown loyalty to the Black community as a whole? According to Oscar, Manager, 53, "Obama has not shown the type of allegiance to Black Americans as we have for him. We have elected this man twice; what has he done for Black America? Look at the voting breakdown in the last two elections." In

2012, Obama received 93 percent of the Black vote. He garnered 96 percent of it in 2008. Clearly, the number of eligible Black voters across the country has overwhelmingly supported Obama in both elections. Oscar further states in his criticism of Obama, "Our support for him is great. I know he is the President of the United States. However, it seems like he is the President more for White America than Black America."

In 2004 at the Democratic National Convention (DNC) while campaigning for presidential hopeful John Kerry, then US Senator Obama was introduced onto the national stage dazzling the American people with his speech. He stated in his closing remarks, "there's not a liberal America and a conservative America—there's the United States of America. There's not a black America and a white America and a Latino America and Asian America—there's the United States of America."[2] Obama's speech embodied great political theater and catapulted the 88th ranked Senator in the US Congress as a potential candidate in the upcoming 2008 presidential election. However, those remarks at the DNC created a breeding ground for controversy prior to the campaign and should have been a sign to come that Obama would not address race-specific issues. Hence, he would not make statements regarding policies directly affecting the welfare of the Black community. One of Obama's biggest critics, Tavis Smiley, said in a 2012 *New York Times* interview, "It has, at times, been painful to watch this particular president's calibrated, cautious and sometimes callous treatment of his most loyal constituency."[3]

Smiley's opinion is similar to that of most participants in this study. There are participants who believe Obama pushed a political agenda that "could possibly benefit" Black Americans but, on the other hand, he has made few verbal references to "Black interest" policies central for directly uplifting those in the Black community. As stated by Bruce, Educator, 41, "What is Obama doing for Black America? We gave him a pass during his first term. Do we know exactly what he has done while in office for Black people? What is the state of Black America? Are we better or worse since he has been in office?"

The election of Obama raised expectations that he would overtly represent the interests of Black Americans. That is, he would address economic, social, and political issues germane to Black constituents. Similar to what other emerging Black politicians had historically done at the local, state, and US congressional level, Black constituents believed he would provide a type of representation that former White presidents of the past had not offered to members of the Black community. However, with no blueprint, how could he know how to *act* as a Black president. Being the first would bring heightened expectations and unknown fears. History had not witnessed the political and legislative behavior of a Black president. How effective would Obama be? How would the Black community measure his effectiveness? Only time will serve as a barometer to measure the presidential leadership and success of Obama. Since he has been in office, has Obama adequately addressed the needs and concerns of Black constituents? Has there been an "Obama Effect" on Black males? Has his presence in office changed the thinking and behavior of Black males? This chapter addresses these questions in an attempt to establish what has been the overall impact of Obama's political actions and societal presence. The aim is twofold: first of all, to identify whether Black males believe that Obama represents the interests of Black constituents as a whole; and second, to explore whether his election and presence has had an impact on Black males.

Are Black Males Voting?

For decades the Black community has been loyal to the Democratic Party. During former president Clinton's election years he received 83 percent of the Black vote in 1992 and 84 percent in 1996. In 2000, when Democrat vice president Al Gore was defeated in an open seat election by

Republican Texas governor George W. Bush, he obtained 90 percent of the Black vote. Even Democratic John Kerry got 88 percent in 2004 in his loss to Bush. Despite the Black community again being loyal to the Democratic Party during Obama's campaign, a significant fraction of Black males were not a part of the political process in 2008 and 2012. Their omission ranged from being disenfranchised due to a felony record, having a felony record prior to developing an interest in voting, which nullified registering, lack of political knowledge about registering to vote, to simply being disinterested in politics.

In 2012 nearly 1.5 million Black males in the United States were not allowed to cast their ballot to vote in the presidential election. State laws restricted their right to vote because they are convicted felons. Black males accounted for 35 percent of disenfranchised voters.[4] Jacob, Self-Employed, 26, explained in his response for not voting for Obama, "I registered to vote when I received my driver's license in high school. A few years later I caught a case [felony conviction]. I like Obama but I just couldn't vote for him." Another participant, Greg, Maintenance Worker, 31, "I am on parole right now, so I can't vote. I didn't vote then [2008] or now [2012]. When Obama got elected the first time I was in prison. Them niggas in prison were going crazy with excitement. We were giving the White guards hell about a Black man being elected as President. Obama made me not want to go back. I wanted to turn my life around."

During the 2012 election period, nine states had lifetime bans on convicted felons. Thirty-two states allowed voting for felons that had served their sentences and finished parole. These felon disenfranchisement laws in many states are outdated. States such as Massachusetts, Maine and Vermont have no felony restrictions.[5] The variety of crimes in which a person can be disenfranchised is wide and varied. In many states, conviction for any crime that warrants imprisonment is basis for disenfranchisement. Less severe examples of crimes that have warranted disenfranchisement range from writing a bad check, gambling, shoplifting, to the disproportionate targeting of Black males for driving while Black (DWB) and misdemeanor drug offenses (Nunn 2005). Corey, Cashier, 29, expressed his reason for not voting, "I went to jail for writing bad checks. Spent my time in jail. Before I went to jail, I registered to vote and even had a voter registration card come to my house. On the day to vote, they swiped my driver's license [at the polling station] and told me I couldn't vote."

Having a legitimate Black candidate for presidential office peaked Blacks' political interest in 2008. This propelled voter registration and turnout among the Black electorate. The number of Black eligible voters increased from 11.6 percent in 2004 to 11.8 percent in 2008. Over one million more Blacks were eligible to vote. An estimated 15.9 million Blacks casted ballots. They had the second highest voter turnout, 65.2 percent behind White voters 66.1 percent. Blacks voted at a higher rate than in any other presidential election in United States history. However, a large percentage of Black males were not registered to vote. Black males 18–24 (43.1 percent) and 25–44 (33.8 percent) represented a significant void in the political process. They lagged considerably behind Black females in casting votes. On Election Day, 68.8 percent of eligible Black female voters supported Obama compared to 60.7 percent of Black males (Lopez and Taylor 2009). For the first time in history, Black females had the highest voter turnout in a presidential election. While we know this gap in vote support is attributed to multiple factors, Black females and younger voters of all races and ethnicities carried the torch of support for Obama, helping enormously in his election bid.

Efforts to understand lower turnout among Black males was voiced by participants in their lack of political knowledge about registering to vote. Ernest, Entrepreneur, 34, stated, "I had never voted in my life before 2012. I honestly believed you could just show up with your driver's license and vote. I did that the last time [2008] and was told I couldn't vote. I had no idea how to register to vote. I never had a reason to vote." Another participant, Bobby, Janitor, 28, indicated in his response that his entire household had no clue about the process of registering to vote. He explained, "My mother and father had never voted. I asked my Aunt how to register but she didn't know either. Luckily, I walked in the post office one day and saw a stack of voter registration forms. We filled them out, got our [voter registration] cards back and voted. It was one of the happiest days in my parent's life."

Participants mentioned that another contributing factor to a lower turnout among Black males in the 2008 presidential election was a disinterest in the political process, which led to a low level of political efficacy. Simply put, most did not believe that their vote would matter in electing Obama, and others did not care enough to vote. This was the first time in history that a Black male had a legitimate chance to become the President of the United States of America. How could Black males be disengaged in the political process? Sean, Manager, 27, expressed his regret, "I didn't vote in 2008. I wasn't registered. It wasn't until after Obama won that I felt guilty about it. I cried like a lot of people after he won because he looked like me and represented what I could potentially become. I just didn't think that a Black man could win." In contrast, Samuel, Graduate Student, 24, expressed, "I chose not to vote. I stood in line for hours with my girlfriend. I eventually decided to leave. She stayed in line. She was pro-Obama, but I wasn't that impressed by him. He seemed like a figurehead. I didn't think White people would vote for him. Plus, I'm not a fan of politics. The system is not designed to help Black males."

The majority of Black males in this study voted for Obama in both election cycles even though dissatisfied with the type of representation provided to the Black community. Lawrence, Entrepreneur, 25, expressed his reason for voting for Obama again in 2012, "I voted for Obama because he needs time to accomplish his policy goals. He has not done a superb job in office. But overall he has done a fair job. I believe he needs a full eight years to clean up [George W.] Bush's mess." Another participant, Kerry, Educator, 32, added, "Of course I voted for Obama again. These White folks crazy if they think Obama can fix the country in four years. Negro, please. I wish he could run again, I would vote for him a third time."

Other participants had more pointed criticism of Obama's lack of representation for the Black community. Ted, Manager, 43, stated:

> I voted for Obama this time around [2012] to continue to do my part. I am highly critical of him at times. For one, he doesn't represent the interests of the Black community. I am tired of people saying he is everyone's president not just Black people. White people have had 43 presidents. Can we just have one that looks out for us. I am not talking handouts. I heard Republicans saying that Obama was buying votes with welfare handouts. That simply was not true. I want Obama to work to lower the unemployment rate for Black men. That would help the Black community as a whole.

Some Black males were flat out disappointed with Obama. For example, Henry, Self-Employed, 37, makes his frustration clear:

> Obama is a coward. He always tries to talk tough to the Black community but is a coward when it comes to the White community. He is always telling Black people we need to stop crying and work harder. Tell those White folks that when they slam you every chance they get. Tell [Karl] Rove and [Donald] Trump that. He's scared of them. I wish I could sit down with him and ask what is he going to do for the Black community in these next four years.

A consistent concern that emerged among participants while discussing whether Black Americans have gotten more or less than they deserve with Obama in office was that they were displeased that he had not pushed more "Black interest" policies in his first term to uplift the Black community.

Therefore, a discussion of "Black interests" is important to decipher why this political agenda is essential to provide Black constituents with a type of representation that is most advantageous to their economic, social, and political plight.

Representing "Black Interests"

Historically, social scientists have provided measures of group interests that are generalizable to all racial and ethnic groups, based on socioeconomic indicators such as unemployment, poverty rates, levels of income, and educational levels (see Sargent 1991; Swain 1993). However, in the case of Blacks, specific measures are important to consider when defining "Black interests." The legacy of slavery, "separate but equal" accommodations, Jim Crow laws, disenfranchisement of Black voters, continued cycles of poverty, and different political cultures among Blacks are important in deciphering "Black interests." These factors provide background in determining what policy areas are vital to the Black community as a whole. The identification of "Black interest" bills can be problematic. According to Kerry Haynie (2001, 19) in his book *African-American Legislators in the American States*, which examines the political and legislative behavior of these legislators, "determining or designating a group's interests is usually a complex and complicated undertaking." David Canon (1999) argues that there is considerable ambiguity in the identification of "Black interest" bills. Past studies that have examined policy areas important to Blacks have focused on social welfare, health care, housing, job programs, education, voting (Haynie 2001; Nelson 1991; Walton 1985;) and civil rights issues (Herring 1990; Miller 1990).

After the reelection of President Obama, many of the Black males expressed that it would be important for him to make a more concerted effort to advance an agenda that promotes "Black interests" in his second term in office. Cleo, Graduate Student, 25, explained, "I voted for Obama to provide substantive representation for the American people. I must admit many of his policies aim to do that. But in some cases he has missed the target with the Black community. It is seriously time for Obama to present a political agenda that represents the Black community before he leaves office." Cleo asserts that President Obama has provided substantive representation to the American people as a whole. According to Hannah F. Pitkin in her seminal work, *The Concept of Representation*, substantive representation entails acting "in the interest of the represented in a manner that is responsive to them" (1967, 209). That is, substantive representation is achieved when the legislative actions of the representative are congruent with their constituents' opinion on policy issues.

Since the passage of the Voting Rights Act (VRA) of 1965, which reformed discriminatory voting laws and increased the number of eligible Black voters, the discussion on representation for Black Americans has expanded. The number of Black politicians competing for and holding political offices increased significantly. Their inclusion provided an opportunity for the systematic advancement of policy issues important to the Black community.

One of the age-old questions in Black politics is: Does descriptive representation lead to substantive representation? Jane Mansbridge (1999, 628) defines descriptive representatives as "individuals who in their own backgrounds mirror some of the more frequent experiences and outward manifestations of belonging to the group." She explains descriptive representatives as those with similar characteristics as their constituents, such as race, ethnicity, gender, or social class, who are expected to provide them with a better understanding of the interest of their constituents. Mansbridge states that descriptive representation "promote[s] a representative's accurate representation of and commitment to constituents' interests" (629). She argues that Black politicians, for example, are better suited than White politicians to represent the needs and interests of the Black electorate. Black elected officials, therefore, are more likely to provide substantive representation, which should be the overall goal of all politicians.

Similarly, Pitkin defines descriptive representation as "the representative's [politician's] characteristics, on what he is or is like, on being something rather than doing something. The representative does not act for others; he 'stands for' them, by virtue of a correspondence or connection between them, a resemblance or reflection" (61). Pitkin concludes that descriptive representation is limited and does not guarantee that the politician will provide substantive representation for their constituency. In a later study, Swain (1993) states that "descriptive representation of blacks guarantees only black faces and is, at best, an intangible good; substantive representation is by definition real and color blind" (211).

In terms of Obama, the criticism pointed his way by many Black skeptics such as Tavis Smiley and Cornell West about his performance in office is that since being elected he has been just a figurehead for Black Americans and does not provide substantive representation to the Black community. They inquired on multiple media outlets before the 2012 election, would Obama provide the "hope" and "change" as promised in the 2008 election cycle? In 2012, he campaigned to move the country "forward." That message was further highlighted in Obama's victory speech:

> It moves forward because of you. It moves forward because you reaffirmed the spirit that has triumphed over war and depression, the spirit that has lifted this country from the depths of despair to the great heights of hope, the belief that while each of us will pursue our own individual dreams, we are an American family and we rise or fall together as one nation and as one people.[6]

Some participants disagree with Smiley and West's assessment of Obama and believe that he has provided substantive representation to the Black community. Antwan, Educator, 47, explained, " I voted for Obama because I believe he can still bring change. Change is incremental, it does not happen over night. Black people in America need to realize that. We are always blaming others for our own shortcomings. Jonathan, Scientist, 32, agreed by stating, "Black folks need to shut the hell up and let the man do his job. He is the President of the United States not Black America. His *Affordable Care Act* and *Race to the Top* program will help the Black community. He is president of Black and White America."

Table 4.1 displays several major pieces of signed legislation during Obama's first term. In addition to standing as

Table 4.1   Signed Legislation by President Obama, 2009–2012

Legislation	Goal
H.R. 1: The American Recovery and Reinvestment Act of 2009; Public Law 111–5.	To boost the national economy by creating and saving jobs.
H.R. 2: Children's Health Insurance Program Reauthorization Act of 2009; Public Law 111–3.	To provide free or low-cost health coverage for children.
H.R. 1913: Local Law Enforcement Hate Crimes Prevention Act of 2009; Public Law No. 111–86.	Expand previous hate crime law to include crimes motivated by a victim's sexual orientation, gender, or disability, in addition to race, color, religion, or national origin.
H.R. 3590: Patient Protection and Affordable Care Act of 2010; Public Law 111–148.	To maintain reasonable health care rates, college students can remain on parent's plan until 26 years old and provide coverage for low-income and minority populations.
H.R. 4872: The Health Care and Education Affordability Reconciliation Act of 2010; Public Law 111–152.	Increase the amount of Pell Grants for low-income students and make it easier for students to repay outstanding loans after graduating.
S. 1789: Fair Sentencing Act of 2010; Public Law 111–220.	Reduce the previous 100-to-1 ratio disparity to 18-to-1 ratio in the amount of powder cocaine and crack cocaine required for the imposition of a mandatory minimum sentence. It eliminated the five-year mandatory minimum sentence for 5 grams of crack cocaine.
H.R. 4783: Claims Resolution Act of 2010; Public Law 111–291.	Provide funding for Black farmers discriminated against from 1983 to 1997 by the US Department of Agriculture.

Source: http://www.whitehouse.gov.

operative universal laws that would benefit all Americans, these laws carry the potential to have a substantive effect on the Black community. Some pieces of legislation have been successful in their early stages while others have not accomplished their intended goal. Take, for example, the American Recovery and Reinvestment Act of 2009 (ARRA) whose primary goal is to increase employment opportunities for all Americans. Vance Gray (2013), in his study of the impact of the Act on Black and Latino employment, found that it fails to address structural employment and unemployment conditions of Blacks. This finding is consistent with the current high percentage of Black unemployment. Despite the shortcoming of ARRA, Obama later announced the educational initiative, *Race to the Top*, funded by the Department of Education Recovery Act as part of the ARRA and that offers school districts incentives to improve low-performing schools. Advocates of the *Race to the Top* program praise Obama for appropriating funds for such legislation. On the other hand, critics such as the National Urban League argue that few Black and Latino students would ultimately benefit from the program. Obama addressed the criticism:

> So the charge that *Race to the Top* isn't targeted at those young people most in need is absolutely false because lifting up quality for all our children—black, white, Hispanic—that is the central premise of *Race to the Top*. And you can't win one of these grants unless you've got a plan to deal with those schools that are failing and those young people who aren't doing well.[7]

As stated in chapter three, the adverse effect of this act has led to closure of low-performing schools in Black and Latino communities.

Obama signed other legislation that definitely falls in the margins of "Black interests." In particular, the Fair Sentencing Act of 2010 addressed a blatant problem of racial bias in federal sentencing. The new law reduced the disparity in mandatory minimum prison sentences for crimes involving crack versus powder cocaine. It dismantled the previous

100-to-1 ratio to 18-to-1. The previous law mandated under the Anti-Drug Abuse Act of 1986, that 5 grams (about one-sixth of an ounce) of crack cocaine is equivalent to 500 grams (about a pound) of powder cocaine, both warranting the same mandatory minimum sentence of five years. These sentences have had a drastic effect on the Black community. According to the US Sentencing Commission, in 2009, 79 percent of the 5,669 sentenced crack cocaine offenders were Black in comparison to only 10 percent of Whites and 10 percent of Hispanics.[8] From 1986 to 2010, almost 82 percent of those convicted for federal crack cocaine offenses were Blacks compared to only 8 percent of Whites. In 2007, as a US Senate member, Obama addressed this disparity by stating, "let's not make the punishment for crack cocaine that much more severe than the punishment for powder cocaine when the real difference between the two is the skin color of the people using them."[9]

One of Obama's signature legislative achievements is the Patient Protection and Affordable Care Act of 2010. The goal of this legislation is to make health care insurance more accessible and affordable. It is geared toward the more than 47 million Americans without health care insurance. In spite of its perceived benefits, this legislation has been met with great opposition from Republicans and Tea Party members since signed into law and in 2013 led to a government shut down. Many label the act as "ObamaCare," arguing that it is a "socialist" piece of legislation because it provides universal health care and further rewards racial and ethnic minorities that depend on governmental assistance. Even renowned Black physician Dr. Ben Carson called ObamaCare, "the worst thing that has happened in this nation since slavery."[10] The Centers for Disease Control and Prevention (CDC) identified in a 2011 report that 18.8 percent of Black Americans under 65 years did not have health insurance coverage. Starting in 2014, this act has the potential to provide nearly seven million Black Americans the opportunity to gain affordable health care insurance.

In the face of Republicans against many of his measures, a Democratic-led Congress from 2009 to 2011 was influential in support of his legislative initiatives. Even with a partisan advantage, Obama did extend an olive branch to Republicans during this period. The president's role in achieving legislative success is highly dependent upon Congress. Partisan support from congressional members is needed to advance his agenda (Bond and Fleisher 1990; Edwards 1980). James, Educator, 49, stressed, "Black folks need to realize that Obama does not make decisions on his own. He has to work with Congress. It is not guaranteed that members of Congress will push his agenda."

During his first term, Obama did attempt to address valence issues shared by all Americans, such as employment, education, and health care. In spite of his efforts, factions of the Black population are not satisfied and do not believe he has helped to improve their current condition. According to a 2013 Pew Research study, Blacks are mixed about their progress since Obama was elected. Only 26 percent of those surveyed believed their situation has improved in the last five years. Almost as many (21 percent) indicate their situation was worse with Obama in office. An overwhelming 51 percent believe the situation is about the same for Black people in this country in the last five years.[11]

One participant, Julius, Stockbroker, 31, conveyed in his response that Obama is well aware of the day-to-day struggles of those in the Black community:

> From the onset of his campaign run in 2008, Obama has had to deal with doubts about his loyalty to the Black community. For someone that started out as a community organizer in Chicago and later became a state legislator, I am sure he is in tune with the needs and concerns of the Black community. Trust me. He knows the problems that exist.

Julius's assertion is correct. Obama is no stranger at pushing an agenda to represent "Black interests." Randolph Burnside and Kami Whitehurst (2007), in their study of Obama's legislative record as an Illinois state senator from the 90th to the 93rd sessions, show that his name is attached to more than 500 bills with the bulk focused in the policy areas of social welfare, health care, education, and criminal justice reform. The authors found, "Senator Obama was the main sponsor on 236 bills introduced in the Senate and more than 40% of these bills were devoted to social welfare issues" (82). He achieved great legislative success as a state senator. For example, in 2003 during the 93rd legislative session, when Democrats took control of the chamber, Obama won General Assembly approval of 26 bills. In the Assembly Obama fancied himself as a staunch liberal who was racially conscious of the needs of the Black community, an image he has desperately avoided during each presidential campaign run.

Deracialization in Obama's Presidential Race

Since the 1960s the type of campaign strategy employed by Black politicians has been important in their election to office. According to Anderson (1997), Black politicians who emerged immediately after the passage of the Voting Rights Act of 1965 were considered "race representatives." They practiced a form of politics that was intended to place matters of race at the forefront of political decisions. The main goal of these politicians was to advance the interests of the Black community.

The Obama camp chose not to racialize their campaign in the first presidential election. They employed a deracialized electoral strategy. McCormick and Jones (1993, 76) define deracialization in the following manner:

> Conducting a campaign in a stylistic fashion that defuses the polarizing effects of race by avoiding explicit reference to race-specific issues, while at the same time emphasizing those issues that are perceived as racially transcendent, thus mobilizing a broad segment of the electorate for purposes of capturing or maintaining public office.

This strategy requires the elusiveness of making the Black candidates' racial identity transparent in order to mobilize a sizeable percentage of the White voting bloc. It also calls for these candidates to promote universal issues and to project a nonthreatening image to increase the probability of White vote support. Political advisors in the Obama camp believed that implementing a deracialized strategy would be an easy task considering his background. Since his father was African and mother was White, each embodied both elements of Black and White America.

The theory of deracialization emerged in the early 1970s, when several Black mayors won victories in majority White cities. Their victories became central in understanding the importance of avoiding race-specific issues during campaigns in order to gain White crossover voters in biracial elections. The official introduction of the theory was in 1973 by political scientist Charles Hamilton. At a National Urban League meeting, he proposed strategies to best approach the "post-protest" phase of the Civil Rights movement. Hamilton encouraged Black politicians to build race-neutral coalitions, especially with Whites, by addressing issues with broad appeal, such as full employment, which he specifically cites as an important issue facing the Black community, but is equally pressing for Whites.

Huey Perry (1990), in his study of Black electoral politics, explains that the modern emergence of deracialized electoral strategies from theory to practice is generally attributed to the 1989 election cycles, which scholars of Black politics have dubbed as "Black Tuesday." Several Black politicians such as L. Douglas Wilder (state: Virginia), David Dinkins (city: New York, New York), Norman Rice (city: Seattle, Washington), and John Daniels (city: New Haven, Connecticut) all made electoral history proving that the usage of a deracialized electoral strategy was an effective approach to mobilize White voters. As stated by Jason, Journalist, 28, "I understand that in 2008 Obama could not say, 'I want to only represent Black folks,' but damn show us some love. At times it seems like we show him more love than he shows us."

Jason's opinion begins to pinpoints some of the major criticisms of deracialization. In L. Douglas Wilder's 1985 campaign to become lieutenant governor of Virginia, he did not present himself as a Black candidate, but rather focused on issues that appealed to all voters. Dwayne Yancey (1988) in the book *When Hell Froze Over: The Untold Story of Doug Wilder*, states:

> Wilder never mentioned race [in his campaign]. He hammered away at why he was more qualified until the media and white voters finally had to pay attention. But his campaign never took on the aura of a black crusade. But Wilder knew he had to have the redneck and suburban vote to win and he went after it.

Wilder made roughly 80 public appearances and a small percentage of it was made in front of majority Black crowds (Clemons and Jones 1993).

One of the initial waves of criticism against Obama was his absence at the 2007 *State of the Black Union* conference. Tavis Smiley invited Obama to attend, but he chose to skip the event to focus on his presidential campaign. When Obama canceled his appearance, it led to criticism about his commitment to Black Americans by choosing to miss an event that each year invited Black leaders to discuss issues of importance to the Black community. New York Senator and former First Lady Hillary L. Clinton, also a presidential hopeful, attended the event. After Obama was elected to office, Smiley and West embarked on a "poverty tour" that included strong criticism of Obama's lack of representation for the Black community. Each stated while on tour that they have disagreed with Obama's policies and their intent was to get the issue of poverty "higher up on the American agenda" and hold the president more accountable.

In a study of deracialization focusing on ten Black political campaigns from 1989 to 1992, Perry (1996) writes that in order for deracialization to be successfully employed, Black candidates must not give into their natural impulse after being elected to advocate "Black interest" issues. He questions the quality of representation that Black constituents would receive from these politicians. Because deracialization is inconsistent with Black candidates focusing on these types of issues, they might often neglect the interests of their Black constituents and thus alienate this part of the electorate. According to Salamon, Business Manager, 35, who bluntly criticized Obama, "It was cool that Obama did not present himself like a Jessie Jackson or Al Sharpton in the presidential race. But, here we are three years in [2011] and I honestly do not know what he has done for Black people. I'm not sure if I will vote for him in 2012."

After Obama's reelection, West along with Smiley gave harsh post-election remarks in an interview with Amy Goodman on the news show *Democracy Now!*. West described Obama as a "Rockefeller Republican in blackface" for being derelict in addressing "Black interest" issues in his campaign such as poverty, the warehousing of Black males in the correctional system, and privatizing American education. West also took jabs at other Black scholars and politicians who support Obama. He expressed, "I love Brother Mike [Eric] Dyson too but we're living in a society where everybody is up for sale. Everything is up for sale. And he and Brother [Al] Sharpton and Sister Melissa [Harris-Perry] and others, they have sold their souls for a mess of Obama pottage."[12]

Jerry, Entrepreneur, 53, takes issue with the constant criticism from West and Smiley. He explained their actions as, "Crabs in a barrel. They just want to stay in the news and be relevant. Black people were poor before Obama and they will be poor after Obama. Give him eight years like you gave [George W.] Bush and he will make some prominent changes." Educator Marc Lamont Hill offered a less critical perspective, but also called for accountability of Obama on the Black Entertainment Television (BET) show *Sleep Talkers*, hosted by T. J. Holmes. He too challenged Black voters to demand substantive change. Hill stated, "If we give somebody 93% of our vote and don't ask for anything, we're not a political movement, we're a fan club."[13]

In the 2012 presidential race, President Obama appeared to make a concerted effort to reach out to more Black outlets to capture the Black vote, despite the criticism from Smiley, West, and other Black political pundits for not representing the Black community. Early on, he visibly pushed for Latino, gay, and women's votes, but not the Black vote. Weeks before the November 6 election, he reached out to Black preachers and Black media outlets to ensure the Black vote, a strategic political move not exercised in the first campaign. The Black and Latino vote were crucial in President Obama's reelection. Flagrant public disrespect of Obama by Tea Party Republicans, constant Republican ridicule referring to him as a "food stamp president," and attempted voter suppression in some red states during the 2012 election motivated some minority groups to support him. In addition to receiving 93 percent of the Black vote, he obtained 71 percent of the Latino vote and 55 percent of all female votes. For the second straight election, the Black vote came at a very low political cost, with no direct promises to Black America. This was despite Romney claiming a week after the election that Obama won reelection by promising policy "gifts" to young and minority voters in the form of forgiveness for college loan interest, free health care for Blacks and Hispanics, and amnesty for children of illegal immigrants. Marcus, Educator, 49, articulated, "I am happy to see the president reelected. I am expecting that in his second term he will do more for the Black community. What does he have to lose at this point? He needs to leave a legacy that will last for generations to come."

THE "OBAMA EFFECT"

The election of Obama as president of the United States was the embodiment of the "dream" the Rev. Dr. Martin Luther King discussed in his "I Have a Dream" speech. Obama's election was a major contribution to the fading identity and mission of the Civil Right movement. We saw in 2008 that young voters of all races, creeds and colors supported Obama. He had an effect on many Americans. According to Raymond, Student, 19, "Obama inspired me to graduate from high school and go to college. He is my role model." In comparison, Donnis, Retired, 71, echoed, "I never thought I'd see the day that a Black man be elected as president of the United States. I wish this had happened earlier in my life so I can fully reap the benefits of his impact. He is a role model for the Black male community."

Obama's story represents the twenty-first century's face of Black male achievement: from being the first Black president, the third Black senator elected to the US Senate since Reconstruction, to the first Black president of the Harvard Law Review. The self-described "skinny guy with the funny name" overcame tremendous odds to rise to national prominence. However, what has been Obama's effect on the masses of the Black male population? Has his presence in office changed the thinking and behavior of Black males? Or is this merely a symbolic achievement? How do we adequately measure his effect? Or is this an immeasurable phenomenon?

The aforementioned literature would signify that the economic and social conditions of the masses of Black males have not improved since Obama was elected. As previously mentioned, they continue to be policed at an alarming percentage, disproportionately incarcerated, unemployment is soaring, poverty rate up, education gap widening, more fathers are absent from the home, and Black males keep killing one another.

Previous studies that have examined the "Obama Effect" explore whether his presence has led to increased academic performance by Black students (Aronson, Jannone, McGlone, and Johnson-Campbell, 2009; Marx, Ko, and Friedman 2009; Smith 2011), whereas others have investigated whether his presence as a Black president has been influential in minimizing racial stereotypes and biases against Blacks (Goldman

2010; Welch and Sigelman 2011). While these studies are essential in assessing Obama's impact on Blacks and Whites, the mixed results offered are limited in their scope of his overall impact. Absent is the attempt to explore all aspects of the contextual effects of Obama's presence, and whether he has or has not motivated large segments of the Black male population to work harder to achieve success. In fact, Aronson et al. (2009) in their study failed to find an "Obama Effect," and concluded that his impact may be limited to a certain Black male populace.

Another important component in evaluating the "Obama Effect" should include optimism of whether Obama's presence in office motivates Black males to work harder to achieve success. The notion of an "Obama Effect" is queried by asking the following question: *Would you say that the election and presence of President Barack H. Obama, as the first Black president, has motivated you to work harder or about the same to achieve success?* The majority of participants (77 percent) responded that the election of Obama motivated them to work about the same. Only 23 percent expressed that his election motivated them to work harder. Most participants "like" Obama and believed he is a "role model" for Black males, but his election did not have any impact on motivating them to work harder. Consider the point of view of Issac, Construction Worker, 37:

> I like Obama. But I can't say he has motivated me to work harder. When I see Obama, I honestly see someone I cannot relate to. He graduated from college. I didn't even graduate from high school. Our paths were different. I'm from the hood. He's from Hawaii. He doesn't know the first thing about growing up in the hood. He doesn't know what it is like to be the man of the house at 15. I was selling dope at 15. I helped my momma buy a car at 16. I've been working hard all my life. What does Obama know about these streets? What does he know about taking care of a family at a young age? So no, he didn't motivate me to work harder. My situation at home motivated me to work harder. I believe it's like that for most Black males where I'm from.

The following participants also informed that Obama's election and presence had not motivated them to work any harder to achieve success:

> *Anthony, Social Worker, 35*: Obama getting elected did not motivate me as far as my own work ethic is concerned. Him being elected, as president, had no direct effect on my life. Not at all. My motivation to work harder is based on my own personal circumstances that existed before he was elected president.
>
> *Derrick, Railroad Engineer, 41*: His election has not motivated me whatsoever. It has only caused me to be more aware of what the government is doing.
>
> I listen to what the "others" complain about regarding him. I'm not an Obama supporter but I do speak up when someone's comments against him are racially motivated.
>
> *Jade, Personal Trainer, 30*: I'm a hard worker in general. Having a Black president doesn't motivate me to work harder. Having a Black father that worked hard all his life is what motivates me to work hard.

Those in the minority who responded that the election of Obama has motivated them to work harder provided positive comments. Eddie, Student, 20, responded, "President Obama has inspired me to become a pharmacist. His influence started in high school. I was S.G.A. [Student Government Association] president and graduated salutatorian. Whenever I feel overwhelmed, he is my inspiration." Another student, Jeremy, 22, indicated the need for more role models like Obama, "He definitely motivates me to work harder. I was a knucklehead. He made me believe that if he could do it, then I could do it. We honestly need more Black male role models like Obama."

Older participants are optimistic and have faith that Obama's presence will motivate younger Black males to work harder. For them, Obama represents centuries of blood, sweat, and tears of previous Black leaders who paved the way for his election. Ferdinand, Retired, 67, articulated, "I never thought in my lifetime I'd see the day that a Black man be elected as president. If that doesn't motivate young people to work harder, then nothing will."

Younger participants (18–29), especially those in college and recent graduates, and older participants (65+) made up the bulk of those who believe Obama has a positive effect on Black males and encourages them to work harder. Participants 30–64 indicated his election did not provide any added motivation. As Chris, Educator, 47, conveyed, "If I'm under 21, I may agree that the election of Obama has motivated me to work harder. But I'm a middle-aged Black man in White America. If Obama had never come along, I still knew it was important to work hard to provide for my family. I agree his presence provides some extra incentive. However, as a Black man in White America I already knew I had to work twice as hard to be successful."

As a follow-up question, participants were asked whether they believe Obama's presence in office increases Black males' *desire* to achieve success. Again, participants expressed that Obama's presence does not have an impact on their lives. The majority believes that Obama could possibly have an impact on the younger generation of Black males, but participants (30–64) did not believe he had any substantial impact on their lives. Derrick also offered this perspective, "I believe that it provokes the active imagination of the younger generation. However, Black males already in the workforce see that there has been no real 'change' since he has been in office." Sharoye, Banker, 42, agreed, "So many Black males my age are disconnected. Obama does not increase our desire to achieve success. He may increase the desire of my 16-year-old son. That is because since he was 10, Obama is all he has known."

According to William, Health Care Administrator, 44:

I would say both "yes" and "no." For those Black males that are ambitious and resilient enough to embrace the challenge of constantly overcoming obstacles, I would say the answer is "yes." However, for those who have a defeatist and pessimistic attitude the answer is "no." Obama's presence alone cannot increase your desire, it has to be innate.

Possibly a more important conclusion from attempting to build on previous studies of the "Obama Effect" is that the majority of participants agree that his election to office and presence will have more of an impact on the younger generation of Black males. The majority of participants in this study are adamant that there is no "Obama Effect" and if there were it has faded since 2009. Any lingering "Obama Effect" is found among younger participants (18–29), especially those in college and recent graduates. Harvey, Realtor, 41, explained:

> I understand why college students and younger males are excited about Obama. The Black community created this psychological shift for them when we preached that anything is possible if a Black male can become president of the United States. While I agree this is true, I also know that when they face the harsh reality of being a Black male in White America it may not deter their desire, but they'll begin to understand that Obama is just a symbol. His election has not made life easier for us.

The "Obama Effect" is a difficult concept to measure, and almost immeasurable without directly soliciting the opinions of Black males. As previous studies of the "Obama Effect" note, their sample population is difficult to generalize to the masses. Taking the comments of the participants together, I found that the notion of an "Obama Effect" has not had the expected positive influence as initially intended in 2008 to promote Black male achievement. The inquiry of Black males provides insight into an ever-growing concept since Obama's election. However, contrary to conventional expectations, Black males observe him as more of a symbol of success than a model of success they can actually emulate.

Conclusion

This chapter has presented a discussion on whether President Obama provides substantive representation to the Black community, and whether his election and presence have a direct influence on Black males. What emerged was the belief of dual accountability to represent both Black and White America in two distinctive fashions, a complex undertaking for the first Black president whose mission is to represent the American people and not certain factions of constituents. In 2008 when Obama was campaigning, his message of "hope" and "change" seemed to be directed toward Black America, and it raised expectations that he would push race-specific issues during his tenure in office. He made promises to address valence issues for all and for those in the Black community to believe he would ameliorate some of their economic and social conditions. The truth is that despite Obama signing historic pieces of legislation during his first term, the economic and social conditions of Blacks in general have not improved.

Obama has never shied away from being called the "first Black president." But in retrospect, he has never fully embraced the responsibilities of that label. Being the president of the United States does call for one to represent the interests of all Americans. Yet, this should not hinder Obama's ability to address race-related issues, something he has seldom done in office. Participants believe that Obama has "good intentions" and, for the most part, has done a "fairly decent" job representing the interests of the Black community. Two important findings are identified in this chapter. First of all, no consensus was found that Obama provides substantive representation to Black constituents. Second, Black males do not believe his election and presence accounts for an "Obama Effect." While the election of Obama is arguably the greatest single achievement in Black American history, his symbolic and actual power has not had a substantial effect on Black America.

CHAPTER 5

Black Boy Fly

Rap artist Kendrick Lamar in the song *Black Boy Fly* provides a cultural narrative of the Black male subculture. He suggests that Black males live in an American society where they ask themselves daily, "[will] I survive to make it up out this hole in time?" In other words, will Black males be able to overcome structural and cultural factors coupled with historical forms of discrimination before they fall victim to the streets. The song further goes on to speak to the fragile psyche of some of today's Black youth. They grow up in environments that discourage their ambitions, make their goals seem unrealistic, and highlight the struggle of overcoming their circumstances. The first and second verses of the song begin with the lyrics "I used to be jealous" referring to watching other Black males from his neighborhood in Compton, California, elevate beyond their deprived conditions and become successful, such as NBA player Arron Afflalo and rap artist, The Game aka Jayceon T. Taylor. Kendrick's jealousy is not a reflection of envy for their achievements, but rather fear that he would not be able to, as they did, overcome the coercive nature of his social environment. He speaks from the standpoint of understanding that opportunities are limited for Black males in the inner-city. Kendrick ends the song by rapping:

> What am I to do/ When every neighborhood is an obstacle/ And two niggas making it out had never sounded logical/ And three niggas making it out, that's mission impossible/

The story told in the song *Black Boy Fly* is all too familiar to Black males. Even years after the election of the first Black male president, the status of Black males in America is still in question. As the preceding chapters have explained, we have lost a generation of young Black males to lack of education, generational poverty, unemployment, victims of police brutality, participants in Black-on-Black gun violence, gang membership, imprisonment, self-degradation, negative influences in rap music, and a host of other structural and cultural forces that plague the Black community.

The discourse guiding this book has analyzed what it means to be a Black male in the twenty-first century and the impact of living in the Obama era. The goal of each chapter was to provide a frame for understanding the thinking and behavior of Black males. From the responses of participants interviewed, it was discovered: (1) Black males felt that they were still thought of as "invisible" in White America; (2) the cultural identity of the Black male often is stripped to achieve the American Dream; (3) there is a generational shift in Black male identity; (4) misogynist and violent rap lyrics continue to have a negative influence on the Black male culture and create divisiveness among Black males and females; (5) Black-on-Black murders remain an epidemic in the inner- city; (6) the negative perceptions of Black males as criminals, low-skilled, and uneducated continue to plague their plight; and (7) the "Obama Effect" has not had the expected positive influence as initially intended to promote Black male achievement. This final chapter discusses individual strategies to promote more personal responsibility among Black males. What will it take to not lose the forthcoming generation of Black males who continue to need male guidance? What plan of action needs to be in place to prevent negative forces from being pervasive enough to deter them from being successful, productive Black males? What individual strategies can be provided to the younger generation of Black males to deal with the expected institutional and systemic barriers and the subsequent social adjustment of being an active, progressive member in American society?

In this chapter a set of individual strategies are introduced to Black males to adopt and practice to address the negative circumstances they may face in their social environment. This chapter does not focus on or provide specific economic or political strategies. From the dialogue presented earlier, I understand the importance of identifying such strategies; however, the goal of this chapter is to offer strategies that promote individual responsibility. Black males must be influential actors in their overall cultural and social development. These strategies are presented in an effort for Black males to triumph over forms of discrimination that have crippled their progress. Black males have traditionally suffered from structural and cultural factors that have had an adverse impact on their quality of life. Consequently, this further propels the need to introduce specific strategies that are proactive and pinpoint actions of individual responsibility rather than foresee the eradication of institutional and systemic discrimination thought to happen in the mythical idea of a postracial America.

When participants were asked what is the best advice you can give to Black males to achieve success, a number of individual strategies surfaced. These strategies are not exhaustive, but they represent what participants believe to be the best strategies to be practiced by Black males to increase their probability of triumphing over adversity and negative forces.

Don't Be An Absent Black Father

The absent Black father has been noted as the precursor to explain the behavior and actions of generations of Black males. There is a negative unidimensional portrayal of Black males as individuals who abandon their children. The majority of participants identified that this historical pattern must stop. There was a widely held view that young Black males need a father to guide their maturation process into manhood. It is important for Black males to be present in the lives of their sons in order to play an integral role in shaping their masculine identity. Tellen, Psychiatrist, 52, suggested, "The most important advice I can provide is to be a father to your children. The role of the father is the missing piece in predicting and understanding the behavior of young Black men. It's no secret that Black men haven't done the best job raising our children. We need to raise Black boys to become men."

As discussed throughout this book, there are a number of reasons that hinder the ability of Black males to be a viable part of the lives of their children (and the children's mother). However, many of those reasons were simply excuses brought about by poor decision making. The most credible of the reasons for Black males' absence involves not understanding how to break the generational cycle of fatherless Black homes. Zion, Student, 22, and a new father explained, "My advice is that we need to be role models for our sons. I just had a baby. It's the greatest feeling in the world. My father wasn't in my life. It hurt me. I rebelled against my mommy by staying out late, running with the wrong crowd and being disrespectful. I got pinched [arrested] for weed possession a couple of times. I did a little time in juvy [Juvenile Detention Center]. I needed a man to mold me. That is what I plan to do with my son."

Participants overwhelmingly agreed that in order to meet the development needs of young Black males, the father must be a constant in their lives. It is important for fathers to educate and reinforce values that will help to break the generational cycle and extinguish the visceral stereotype of Black males abandoning their parental responsibilities. There is a huge void in the lives of the current generation of Black males who have grown up without their biological fathers. The impact of a father's presence is immeasurable. Black males who neglect their duty to raise their sons contribute to the dysfunctional cycle that continues to permeate in the Black family, propels the victim-laden identity that many Black males adopt, and leave their sons to grasp for a masculine model of success.

Understanding Black Masculinity

There is a poignant scene in the 1992 movie *Malcolm X*, when Brother Baines of the Nation of Islam (NOI) is attempting to recruit Malcolm into the religious group. He tells Malcolm, "I think you got more sense than any cat in this prison. But why the hell don't you use it?...You go bustin' your fists against a stone wall. You're not usin' your brain. That's what the white man wants you to do...What makes you ashamed of bein' black?" Toward the end of this heated exchange Malcolm asks Brother Baines, "Man, who are you?" Brother Baines replies, "No! The question is, who are you?"

Malcolm X is the epitome of Black masculinity. This prolific scene precedes the cultural transformation of a Black man born as Malcolm Little, whose father dies at a young age and he is left to frame his own idea of Black masculinity. He transitions from a street hustler known as Detroit Red to eventually become a national Black leader. His life identifies the process of cultural transformation that many Black males go through in their life span to find and secure a sense of Black masculinity. For Malcolm, it began with a personal pledge ascribed by the doctrine of the NOI to become a Black male who understood the trials of Black life, to fight against injustices, and to display honor, dignity, and respect as a member of the NOI. Despite making anti-White and anti-American remarks early in his leadership with the NOI, he learned from those mistakes and later forged unilateral relationships with members of all racial and ethnic groups. This is not to imply that Black males have to be members of the NOI to realize the layers of Black masculinity, but like Malcolm's exchange with Brother Baines, there must be a point of enlightenment.

In his advice to Black males, Thomas, Contractor, 31, suggested that they should "understand what it means to be a Black man." He used Malcolm X as an example by saying, "The Malcolm X we read about in history books is not the person that died in [February 21] 1965. The person that died that day was El-Hajj Malik El-Shabazz. Malcolm X died a changed man." Thomas went on to describe his personal time spent in jail and how it provided him with a different perspective of what it means to be a Black man:

> I am not the man today that I was ten years ago. No one ever taught me how to be a man, especially a Black man. That comes with a whole set of additional factors to learn about. I did some time in jail. Those six months gave me more perspective on life. Like I said, I read the *Autobiography of Malcolm X*. The book taught me how the system emasculates Black males. It did back then and continues to do the same today. White America marginalizes Black males. We have to define a role for ourselves to overcome it.

Andrea G. Hunter and James E. Davis (1994), in their study of the complexity of Black masculinity, argue, "what Black men are and what they should be is measured against the status and privilege of White males. The result is that we know little about how Black men define themselves" (20). As a consequence, Black masculinity is a difficult concept to define without juxtaposing it with the concept of White masculinity where the role is more traditional and conventional and without the same plight. Percy, Retired Educator, 69, expressed in his response:

> As a society, we believe that the struggles of all men are the same. I didn't grow up like men of other races and ethnicities. My struggle was different. My development came in stages. My identity as a Black man evolved over time. I went from a sheltered Black kid, to radical Black college student, to diplomatic Black employee in the academic world, to now just an old Black man that wants to enjoy the rest of his days.

According to Herman, Barber, 41, "The best advice I can give young dudes is to learn their history. They need to know what it means to be a Black man in America. This is a hard job. If you do not have a father in your life, there are no instructions on how to be successful at it." Along the same line, Percy, indicated, "My job as a father raising a son was two-fold. First, I needed to teach my son what it meant to be a man; to be a father and provider for his family. Then I needed to teach him what it meant to be a Black man. We face certain life-altering experiences that other races, ethnicities and genders do not face." The crisis of understanding Black masculinity is a continuum in the Black male subculture. How we frame Black masculinity in the Obama era is crucial to restoring more progressive images of the masses of Black males who are in the day-to-day struggle of accepting challenges and overcoming circumstances with the shadow of Obama lingering of what American society believes should be the ideal of Black masculinity.

There Is No Uniform Definition of "Blackness"

The challenges Black males face provide an important vantage point on the intersections of race, ethnicity, and gender. Deep-rooted in the exploration of Black masculinity is the alleged depth of an individual's "Blackness." What is Blackness? How is it measured? Is Blackness the juxtaposition of Whiteness? As discussed in Chapter One, those in the Black community even questioned the validity of President Obama's Blackness. What constitutes an acceptable degree of Blackness for those in the Black community? Are there specific cultural rituals that need to be performed to gain acceptance? Has the need to gain more Blackness for cultural acceptance been a liability for most Black males? The short answer is, yes.

According to Teodre, Mechanic, 58, "My advice would be to be true to yourself. You don't have to be hardcore, a hood dude, a real nigga, or whatever saying these young men use. Be an authentic Black man. Be like Obama. He is a good role model. But they say he is not Black enough." In the same vein, Kevon, Educator, 44, indicated, "There is no one definition of Blackness. We have moved into a 'post-Blackness era.' Black people, particular Black males, are not a monolithic group. They don't all listen to rap music, commit crimes or are lazy members of society. Don't feed into the stereotype and peer pressure. Black males can display intelligence and perform activities that are abnormal to those in the Black community. But most want to be 'real niggas' rather than productive members of society."

Kevon echoes a point made by participants that young Black males (and older) have a narrow perspective of what it means to be "Black." Blackness is a complex self-described identity. There are inherent dangers that arise when Black males narrow the scope of what it means to be Black and succumb to cultural pressures. Individuality can help alleviate irrational thinking that sometimes leads Black males to participant in deviant activities. For instance, the faulty notion that Black males from affluent families, who go to private schools, speak proper dialect, and become successful do not have enough obvious Black cultural markers to be considered "Black enough." However, on the other hand, those that come from poverty, raised in single-parent households, barely graduate from high school, either go to jail or nearly face death are "Legitimately Black." An unacceptable percentage of Black males think in this manner. The concept of Blackness should have a positive, achievement-laden frame of reference.

The extent of Black maleness is bundled in an oppressive history, which makes each layer difficult to peel back and examine thoroughly. The swinging pendulum between being considered an "Uncle Tom" to "Successful Black Man" to "Angry Black Man" to "Real Nigga" mirrors that of W. E. B. DuBois's "warring soul" as Black males are faced with the day-to-day realities of living in a subculture that challenges their manhood and Blackness. The younger generations of Black males will learn the meaning of Blackness from their parents and peers. Thus, the Black community as a whole must widen its perspective of Blackness and understand that the ideas of individuality and multiplicity are essential to their plight and level of achievement.

A Post-Racial America Does Not Exist

In spite of the welcome positive image of President Obama as a model of racial progress, participants agreed that there appears to be a heightened level of covert discrimination and racism toward them since his election. According to Jermaine, Former Professional Athlete, 41, "Obama made racism worse. After he was elected, I received more nasty looks and folks made snide remarks toward me. It was almost as if they saw me as Obama." Participants believed that "Obama haters," "Conservatives," and "Republicans" interacted with them in a negative way. They made clear that Black males do not live in a unified post-racial American society. Gerald, Entrepreneur, 36, stated, "I'm a big Obama fan, but the belief that his election has led to a post-racial America is nonsense. Walk a day in my shoes. You will see that a post-racial America does not and will never exist, especially for Black males." All participants who offered their opinion of whether a post-racial society exists for Black males endorsed these sentiments. Gerald went on to state, "The ability to not consider race when I walk out of my door every morning is a luxury that only White Americans have been afforded."

Some participants took a historical stance to affirm that a post-racial America does not exist for Black males. Rena, Educator, 52, explained, "Racism has historically been embedded in the cultural and social fabric of the United States. White supremacist practices continue to be systemically a part of the social construct. That was evident when Obama ran for office in 2008." During Obama's 2008 campaign, GOP members, Tea Party members, and misguided Americans displayed and voiced their racial ignorance. Videos and picture images surfaced on the Internet and at Tea Party rallies that depicted Obama and his family as monkeys, and campaigners held signs that read "Obama's Plan, White Slavery," "The New Face of Hitler," "Show Us Your Birth Certificate," "Slave Owner Tax Payer = Niggar," and "Save White America." These overt racial messages drove the notion that a segment of the White American population still harbored remnants of discrimination and racism.

While much of the dislike toward Obama is fueled by politics, the majority of participants strongly believed that the White hatred toward him is racially driven and creates a social landscape where Whites continue to hold racial feelings that have trickled down from past centuries. Some participants strongly believed Obama's election and presence deepened racial divisions. For example, Jason, Journalist, 28, expressed, "These White folks can't stand to see a nigga in the White House. Let's be honest. White folks at my job loved me before Obama was elected. I was always invited to lunch, dinner, weekend events, etc. After he was elected that stopped." Samuel, Graduate Student, 29, summed it up best when pondering the notion of living in a post-racial society by saying, "Allowing young Black males to believe they are living in a post-racial society is a dangerous fallacy. It can be detrimental to their human survival. We are not a color-blind society. I am a Black male and I want you to see that."

Education Is the Pathway to Success

Education is often touted as the pathway to success. Participants believed that a substantial piece of advice for Black males was to seek education as a method to gain success. They also added that some young Black males often do not see the value in education and this thought process began at an early age. There is a cultural frame of reference among Black males that being educated is "not cool" and academic achievement is "synonymous with acting White." As stated by Cameron, Student, 21, "My parents always told me to get an education. Both of my parents graduated from college. But most people are not like us. When I go home for Christmas and summer breaks, my homeboys make fun of me. They say, 'you a school boy' or 'you think you're better than us.' It's not my fault they didn't go to college. We all graduated [from high school] together." When asked to further explain how these comments from friends made him feel, he described, "In high school it affected me. I use to bomb tests on purpose and suppress my intelligence in class during discussion group to fit in."

When participants did not identify education as advice they would give to Black males, they were probed about the value of education. Some offered the viewpoint that "common sense" is key. In addition to devaluing education, some Black males believed that common sense was more advantageous than book sense. John, Maintenance Worker, 39, explained, "School is not for everyone. Education is cool, but you have to know how to hustle. I am not talking about anything illegal, just have a skill to make money." Others identified how education does not increase earning potential. Cole, Entrepreneur, 28, argued that school has no value, "I dropped out of school. But, I have a home, nice whip [car], and can buy anything I want. I make more money than people with degrees. I don't want to sound like I am dissing education, but you don't need it to be successful." While valid on a case-by-case basis, Cole's passionate argument regarding education is not applicable to the mass Black male population.

There is a sizable gap in educational success among Black males and other demographics as talked about in this book, which was of grave concern to participants. Aaron, Lawyer, 28, expressed, "We need to educate Black males and close the [educational] gap. Education saved my life and I am sure it can do the same for more Black males." In general, the educational expectation for Black males needs to increase. Education is cool. Being smart is not synonymous with acting White. Not all Black males are natural born hustlers. Black males must move beyond a way of thinking that continues to erode their negative perspective of education and work to achieve academically.

We Must Not Devalue Black Male Life

"Y'all wanna see a dead body?" is one of the most undervalued quotes in the history of Black cinema. This quote comes from the 1991 film *Boyz n the Hood*. The film takes a glimpse into the world of young Black males raised in the inner-city of Los Angeles. In this particular scene, a group of four young Black males are gallivanting about, killing time, when one says to the others, "Y'all wanna see a dead body?" After a slight pause one of the young males replies, "Yeah." This scene captures a sad but true reality among Black males. Some are unemotionally affected by the loss of Black male life. From birth to their unexpected or untimely death, loss of life is accepted and compartmentalized as the harsh reality of being a Black male. The director, John Singleton, magnifies this point in the scene by making the discovery of the dead Black male body by a group of young Black males. Their reactions were subtle and inquisitive. They spoke among themselves, "Lookin' like Freddy Kreuger got him," "He stank," and "I wonder why it takes them people so long to pick him up?" When a group of older Black males discover them viewing the body, one of the young Black males yells to them, "Don't you know this is a dead body?" A member from the older group replied, "Yeah motherfucka, I know that shit. He ain't bothering you, so don't fuck with him." The summation of this scene shows the generational effect of devaluing Black male life.

Participants expressed that in the Black community they were taught that the lives of young Black males has never held great value in the United States. There already exists an ideology that Black male life is worthless due to racial profiling, police vigilance toward Black males, high rates of arrest, and incarceration. Understanding this societal epidemic, we should not see more Black males contribute to the death of other Black males. Salamon, Business Manager, 35, defends this positions by stating, "My advice to Black males is to not be a participant in Black-on-Black murders. When the perpetrator and victim are Black, that is a hard pill to swallow."

What is the value of Black male life? Do Black males know their own self-worth? Would greater insight into their own self-worth diminish the overall number of Black-on-Black murders in this country? Jobai, Graduate Student, 31, offers this opinion on the value of Black male life. He stated:

> My advice is for Black males to understand that they are Kings. We've gone from pyramids to projects. We need to re-establish our self-worth. That starts by loving each other. We are mentally enslaved to believe that our Black brothers are the enemy. They are not the enemy. The enemy is "self." Because we do not understand that, we kill those that look like us, I fear that one day another Black man will kill me.

Don't Be a Bull's-Eye

Trayvon Martin is an American metaphor. His death, like that of other Black males who have died at the hands of over-zealous law enforcement figures in positions of authority or power, symbolizes the continued devaluation of Black male life. In early 2012, George Zimmerman, a neighborhood watch patrol officer, fatally shot Trayvon Martin while he was returning home from a local convenience store. Zimmerman reported to the 911 operator before the death of Martin that there had been "some break-ins" in the neighborhood and Martin looked "suspicious." According to one participant, Trayvon Martin's death while tragic could have been avoided. Warner, Banker, 33, stated, "My advice to Black males would be to avoid the bullshit. You know you are a moving target in White America. Don't be a welcomed moving target. I'll say this and it won't be favorable among Black people but Trayvon Martin was partly to blame for his own death."

Warner proceeded to pinpoint specifics of the supposed confrontation between Martin and Zimmerman. He described some competing events leading up to Martin's death. First, Zimmerman should have never exited his vehicle. Second, Zimmerman was told by the 911 operator not to pursue Martin and allow the police to handle the matter. He disobeyed a direct order. Third, Zimmerman racially profiled Martin. At one exchange with the 911 operator, Zimmerman said, "These assholes they always get away." Last, and his most important point, Martin could have identified himself and resolved the suspicion. Warner then posed a reflective question, "Why didn't Trayvon Martin identify himself? Was that the time to be a martyr for the cause? No. The truth is that Trayvon was a troubled young man. He needed help. He needed male guidance in his life. If George Zimmerman didn't kill him, he would have been killed eventually or went to jail. He was headed down that path."

During the time of his death, Martin was visiting his father. His mother had kicked him out of the house after being suspended from school for ten days for carrying a baggie that contained marijuana residue. It was the third time Martin was suspended in the school year. On one occasion, Martin was suspended for writing W.T.F. on a hallway locker, the acronym for (W)hat.(T)he.(F)uck. The next day, a search of his book bag found women's jewelry and a screwdriver. School officials presumed that the jewelry was stolen.

Warner further goes on to express, "I introduce these different situations because it speaks to the double entendre that we empower young White boys and make young Black boys feel powerless. Black boys are in a lose-lose situation. My advice is do not become a moving target. When they do society puts a big bull's-eye on their back." His recommendation to Black males opened a debate among those interviewed afterward. Some participants were probed about whether they believed Martin's death could have been avoided if he had identified himself. Anthony, Social Worker, 35, argued:

> My feelings are that you don't have to be submissive to blatant harassment. Trayvon defended himself. Now he is dead. The media demonized him. Yes, he smoked weed, took offensive pictures, got suspended from school and inquired about buying a gun. He was being a teenager, not a bull's-eye. When I looked at the photo of his dead body, what stays with me is that here was a kid wearing a hoodie that went to the store to buy Arizona Ice Tea and Skittles and now he is dead. He could have grown up to be a productive, contributing member of society.

Vonn, Educator, 26, took a similar position. He explained:

> I understand the argument. Let's be clear, Trayvon is not responsible for his own death. He didn't deserve to die; Not under any circumstances. Was he becoming a bull's-eye in his life? Yes. Was he a bull's-eye that night? We don't know. History tells us that Black males are born bull's-eyes. Trayvon was like most young Black males that smoke weed all day, pants saggin and do all kinds of dumb shit. We need to teach them how to make better decisions with their life.

The double negative is that certain factions of White America do not value Black male life and some Black males do not value their own lives. To help resolve these negatives into a positive, Black males can no longer be "bull's-eyes" to a system designed to shoot first, and ask questions later. As summed by Larry, Academic Advisor, 41, "We must remain hyperaware of our surroundings. It is important to present ourselves in a manner that doesn't disgrace our ancestry. Our actions cause a reaction. We must make decisions to offset potential harm."

Predict the Behavior of the Oppressor

"Predict the behavior of the oppressor." The late Dr. William R. Jones, professor of African American studies and religion at Florida State University (FSU), used to always relay this message to his Black students. I met Dr. Jones in the summer of 1997 prior to my first year in graduate school at FSU in a Black graduate student orientation program (BGSOP). He conducted a seminar session explaining his JAM and JOG oppression models. Each was an acronym: Jones Analytic Model (JAM) and Jones Oppression Grid (JOG). Dr. Jones supplied students with note excerpts from his unpublished manuscript, *Oppression-Centric Pedagogy 101: A Reference Manual and Workbook*, which details the models. These models were designed to navigate through the No Parity, No Prosperity (NPNP) minefield that sets traps for Black

folks to fail. He laid out the contextual and situation vari-
ables in each model to respond to oppression at the micro-
and macrolevels.

Many years later, I still remember two important phrases
imparted by Dr. Jones (still written in my collection of notes
from 1997): "Predict the behavior of the oppressor," and "If
you don't understand oppression, you will be oppressed." He
stressed that it was our responsibility, as Black Americans, to
figure out the intent of the oppressor and decode the multiple facets of oppression. Dr. Jones noted that the symbol of
the oppressor does not absolutely mean "the White man."
He provided a simplistic definition of oppression, "the origin of difference; unjust treatment by anyone in an superior
position." Any human being, regardless of race or ethnicity, can oppress another. In some cases, Blacks oppress other
Blacks. However, as it relates to Whites, many have been
given a surplus of institutional powers and privileges that
allot them the ability to oppress other groups or subgroups.
Participants declared it was imperative for Black males to have
a heightened level of awareness and understanding of oppression when adjusting in predominantly White environments.
Floyd, Entrepreneur, 47, expressed, "White folks are playing
a game that some Black folks still have not been able to figure
out. Black males have to be strategic, educate ourselves, maximize our resources and assimilate without selling out. Our
thinking needs to be two to three steps ahead when interacting with White folks. This is not condescending advice but
important advice for the success of Black males. Some of us
are being oppressed everyday and do not know it."

Participants believed that predicting the behavioral traits
of Whites is necessary and vital for the continued plight of
Black males. According to Sean, Manager, 27, "I don't trust
White people. I'm the only Black manager at my job. It took
me a while to understand that they will always do what is in
their best interest. Each day when I get to work, I feel like I
have to gauge the climate of the workplace. I have to be extra
nice, more attentive, present my ideas in a non-threatening

manner and figure out who actually has my best interest."
To affirm Sean's point, Black males must work to predict the
behavior of the oppressor and not be oppressed. It is important for them to decode the multiple facets of oppression.
Lack of knowledge and awareness among Black males will
continue the thriving nature of oppression.

Stop "Keepin' It Real"

For Black males, the mantra "Keepin' it Real"—or words to
that effect—has had an adverse effect. Thought to exult posi-
tivity in the minds of Black males, this slang term has been
harmful to their progress. "Keepin' it Real" is a multifaceted
phrase. It is often defined as being a straight shooter, very
honest among friends, remembering where you come from
(i.e., attached to your community, neighborhood, etc.), and
staying loyal to past and current friends who lead a criminal
or troublesome lifestyle. Many participants believed this to
be true of most Black males. The downside to "Keepin' it
Real" is that in many cases, it has an undesirable outcome.
They are unable (and sometimes unwilling) to break the
bond of negativity that exists because they feel obligated to
"Keep it Real." Dylan, Minister, 34, argued that, "the best
advice for young Black males is to surround themselves with
like-minded people. Leave the past friends alone that will
compromise their dreams and goals."

Black males have an inexplicable attachment to the "friends
they grew up with." It is a kind of solidarity that at times
will lead the progressive friend to compromise his pursuit
of success in fear of breaking the unwritten code and being
called a "Sellout." Diop, Self-Employed, 44, explained, "My
advice is to drop the dead weight. One of my biggest regrets
was having so-called friends around me when I was playing
basketball in college. My boys from back home would come
to campus and bring weed. The [head] coach found out
and kicked me off the team." Harold, Supervisor, 37, told a
similar story of being temporarily dismissed from his college

football team. He stated, "My advice is to assess your friendships…I was too loyal to my friends from the crib. They'd come stay [with me] for a week [on campus]. I would miss class, study hall and was late to practice. Then I failed a drug test. I was dismissed from the team for a while. My dream of playing college football was almost taken from me."

The phrase "Keepin' it Real" is strongly associated with some in the Black male subculture. What seems like passive slang to the general population is a way of life. This is similar to what Elijah Anderson (1999) in the book *Code of the Streets* describes as an unwritten code among Black males. The main problem is that young (and older) Black males have to realize that nothing is "real" about remaining a part of forces of negativity, which compromises their ability to be resilient in the face of individual circumstances. Frankly, they must alleviate themselves from a thinking that promotes criminal or troublesome behavior to appease and honor friendships. The quest is to break the cycle, not to continue it so as to be accepted by peers who have no genuine interest and concern for the welfare of a friend trying to succeed.

Jordan Effect > Obama Effect

In the Black male subculture, the "Jordan Effect" is more powerful than the "Obama Effect." Statistics would reflect that more Black males stand in line for the release of retro Nike Air Jordans than standing in graduation lines to receive their high school and college diplomas combined. The anticipated release dates are often followed by fights, robbery, and in some cases, death. Some Black males put more stake in obtaining Nike Air Jordans than valuing and respecting the humanity of Black male life. According to Landon, Entrepreneur, 37, "[Nike Air] Jordan's and drugs are working a hundred times better than chains and whips. Kayne [West] was right when he said we are the 'New Slaves.'"

The root of Black males' infatuation with the possession of Nike Air Jordans is multilayered and exemplifies deeper structural and cultural wounds. Some are uneducated, impoverished Black males who seek material goods to validate their identity. There is not enough literary space in this section to cover every facet of this epidemic in the Black male subculture. In my opinion, Michael Jordan was a Hall of Famer on the basketball court but off the court he has no moral attachment to the generations of young (and older) Black males who idolized his basketball prowess. He is considered the greatest basketball player of all time. Black males love wearing Nike Air Jordan shoes and apparel, even those who weren't yet born to watch him play. Michael Jordan is an icon in the Black male subculture. His allure and presence is kept relevant through advertising his Nike Air Jordan brand and the rap music culture. References in rap music to "Jordan" or "23" are believed to exemplify the pursuit of greatness.

According to participants, two compelling reasons make the "Jordan Effect" seem to be greater than the "Obama Effect." First, Black males believe it's easier to become a professional athlete than president of the United States. Second, the idea of a Black president is new to the "social consciousness" and "psyche" of Black males. For most Black males, Michael Jordan represents a real life goal. He also reflects the Black male subculture's definition of success. They associate the image of Michael Jordan with attributes of athletics, entertainment, clothing, shoes, women being attracted to men who wear his high-end apparel, and more importantly, less time to be spent in school to become successful. In contrast, President Obama represents having to obtain multiple degrees to become successful and extended time spent in school. For instance, Lewu, Educator, 49, explained, "Black males do not think they can become Obama. It requires too much time in school. However, to be Michael Jordan all you need is a basketball and a hoop. That's the simplicity of their thinking. It disturbs me. I understand that becoming an NBA basketball player is a more attainable goal, but I want these young men to expand their way of thinking."

Over the last two decades, Michael Jordan has been able to amass a fortune from playing basketball, featuring in giant corporate endorsements, starring in movies, and selling the Nike Air Jordan brand. Some participants were concerned that Michael Jordan cares more about making money than the welfare of Black males who desire to obtain his shoes by any means necessary. Harrin, Judge, 53, argued, "The best advice to give to young Black men would be to stop investing in material things like Jordan's. Michael Jordan doesn't care about you nor does he need your money. These shoes were originally released in the 1990s and cost about $50 bucks. Now they are being rereleased twenty years later and cost $200 bucks. We, as Black people, should be ashamed of ourselves."

Harrin went on to say, "Black men need to be accountable for their actions. There should now be no reason why young Black men aspire more to be a professional athlete than President of the United States. I know Michael Jordan can't control the behavior of young Black men. But he can work to reduce the price and lower the public appeal of the shoes. We have to change the savage mentality that makes us kill over Jordan's, but won't kill over change for the socioeconomic position of Black men in this country." I agree with Harrin's position, Michael Jordan shouldn't be held responsible for the lack of judgment or misplaced values of those who participate in unruly and violent acts to obtain his shoes. On the contrary he should be an active participant in finding a solution to ensure public safety when the purchase of the Jordan brand evokes deviant acts among Black males. Michael Jordan was an MVP (Most Valuable Player) on the basketball court; however off the hardwood he has been MIA (Missing In Action) when it comes to being an all-around role model for Black males who still idolize him.

Chase the Realistic Dream, Not the Elusive Nightmare

Young Black males should be taught to dream. And there is nothing wrong with dreaming about becoming a professional athlete, rapper, or some type of entertainer. This is a path many have taken to become successful. However, not every Black male can achieve success in these professions. By far one of the most common pieces of advice was for Black males to have realistic dreams and goals. Very often, Black males believe the only way to become successful is to indulge in sports or entertainment. That simply is not true. As stated by Rico, Educator, 53, "Black males are capable of choosing a career path that does not involve sports or rapping. When they invest in these types of goals, in some ways, it lowers their ambitions. Some believe this road is easier, but it's not. The dream can lead to a nightmare because Black males have invested more time in these mediums than education. You can't play sports forever. Once they do not become LeBron James or Lil Wayne, they become lazy."

Many participants felt that young Black males lacked personal motivation beyond sports and entertainment. Once they fail to rise from anonymity to stardom as an athlete or rap artist, they become stagnant. For many, there is no Plan B. Their dream becomes a nightmare because they believe wholeheartedly that these were their only options to become successful. The lack of personal motivation does not lead them to work hard in pursuit of another career path; especially one that involves education beyond high school. Those expressing this view were not only disgruntled with some Black males lack of personal motivation, but also, how they rationalized their level of stagnation. According to Andre, Engineer, 46, "I'm sick and tired of young Black men saying 'I'm just doing me.' Is that code for, 'I've given up on life?'" In some circles, the phrase, "I'm just doing me" is slang for living your life the way you want to with no societal expectations. It represents complacency, lack of personal accountability, and being plain lazy. Andre added, "When young Black men do not become ballplayers or rappers it seems like they give up on life. They turn to a life of hustling, selling drugs or getting a mediocre job."

The consensus was that some Black males have resisted education as a pathway to success, lowered their level of ambition, found alternate ways to generate income, and are detached from certain societal expectations. Take, for example, one year I was visiting my family during the Thanksgiving holiday. My nephew attempted to make a convincing argument that he was "just doing me" with his life. At the time, he was 26-years-old, staying with his grandparents, had no job, paid no bills, had been arrested several times for marijuana possession, and had a baby on the way with a woman he was unwed to. He attended college for one academic year, but failed out. My nephew spent the bulk of his day being an aspiring rap music producer, hanging with friends, smoking marijuana, and playing video games. When I confronted him about getting his life together, his reply was, "I'm just doing me." He was in pursuit of the elusive nightmare.

Community Mentorship

There are three historical phrases repeatedly used in the Black community to uplift and empower each other. First, "It takes a village to raise a child." Second, "To whom much is given, much is required." Third, "Each one, teach one." Sadly, as a community, some have lost sight of the practice of these phrases. For Black males, in particular, the need to restore the validity of these phrases is imperative for more to become successful. During the interview process, the question was asked: *Do you think that what happens generally to Black people in this country will have something to do with what happens in your life?* to gauge their level of *linked fate*. Linked fate, according to Michael Dawson (1994), is the degree to which an individual believes that his/her own self-interests are linked to the interests of his/her race. He argues that the concept of linked fate "explicitly links perception of self-interest to the perception of the racial group interest" (77). Thus, Blacks who strongly associate themselves with the Black group will be more likely to help others. Unfortunately, most participants indicated they did not believe that what generally happens to Black people in this country will have something to do with what happens in their own lives.

According to Marvin, Contractor, 40, "My advice would be to mentor these young men. Gone are the days when an older cat would say, 'Hey, let me holla at ya.' You knew he was about to impart some wisdom and tell you to get your act together. If you try telling one of these young men something these days, you may end up dead." In his response, Marvin identifies that older and younger Black males do not complement each other through a symbiotic relationship. There is an internal force that pushes them apart and widens the gap between mentor and potential mentee. There is neither the willing dissemination of information nor active seeking of information. But rather, older Black males approach these relationships with the rhetoric and position, "I'm older than you, therefore you need to listen" and younger Black males are likely to respond, "Fuck that old nigga, he don't know shit. Look at how he is living." Much of this deteriorated respect is due to young Black males growing up without a father. They do not always acknowledge that they desire to have a father. As a result, the mentoring gap is often met with resistance. Ikem, Social Worker, 33, explained, "We need to do a better job at mentoring these kids. When you are raised only hearing a mother's voice, you turn a deaf ear to a man trying to tell you what to do."

Black males must recognize that there is a social and moral obligation to reach back and help those less fortunate. It should not be a burden. It should be a privilege. There should exist a growing community of Black male mentors who understand the obligation to uplift and empower each other. This disposition among Black males requires strength. It is to the benefit of the Black male subculture to be a unified, powerful force that mentors and encourages the continual triumph of all Black males. Ariel, Educator, 61, concluded in his response, "My grandfather always use to preach that the one with knowledge and the fool end up in the same place—the graveyard. When an individual understands that, they should be more inclined to help others reach their potential."

Focus on Triumph Rather Than Plight

For the Black community, the term "plight" is synonymous with the economic, social, and political struggle from slavery to present day. Despite the countless triumphs of Black people for centuries, the social identity and cultural frame of the Black race are tied to the struggle of the past. For good or bad, much of this connection is pointed out by Black Americans and often used as an "excuse" or "caveat" to explain failure. As stated by Treven, Entrepreneur, 55, "My advice is for Black males to stop blaming the past. It is not 1619. There is no need to continue to focus on our plight. Only use it as motivation. Slavery happened. It had a devastating impact. There is no doubt about it. But we need to overcome the mentality of blaming current members of White America for slavery." While expressed in different ways, many participants agreed it is essential to recognize past transgressions inflicted on the Black race, but not let the past hinder the pursuit of Black male achievement.

Today, the plight of Black males continues to worsen. Inasmuch as that can be attributed to remnants of slavery, which perpetuates institutional and systemic discrimination, worsening circumstances can be viewed as self-inflicted. Jamie, Lawyer, 32, argued in his response:

> My advice is for Black males to stop making so many damn excuses. The White man is not to blame for your lack of success. It is you. If you don't want to go to prison, act right. If you want a job, go to school and get an education. I was raised in the inner-city. My family was poor. I didn't have a father. I worked hard in school and eventually became a lawyer. Have I experienced racism? Yes. Have I been discriminated against? Yes. A lot of Black males have. And a lot of Black males have become successful.

Black males must work through forms of discrimination and overcome a mentality deeply embedded in the Black culture that reinforces doubt, expects failure, and sees limited opportunities for success. The actual fruition or triumph requires hard work and serious effort. Opportunities are plentiful for Black males once they overcome the fear of working through stages of potential failure and understand that in order to succeed hard work is expected in the face of adversity. For Black males, achievement matters. The preoccupation with plight marginalizes the Black male. He enters into a life of excuses and blame rather than working to restore cultural competency by increasing the rate of achievement for Black males as a whole. Inis, Coach, 38, explained, "No one wants to hear how hard you've had it, they want to know what you have accomplished. As the adage goes, 'If there is no struggle, there is no progress [Frederick Douglass].' I believe that progress can't be made if Black males are always playing the blame game." Throughout history, the hardships experienced by Black males have made them resilient. Hence, past models of Black male success should be used as personal motivation to persevere through the structural and cultural factors that have been a barrier to Black male triumphs.

Obama's Message of "No Excuses"

The election and presence of President Barack H. Obama was to symbolize the twenty-first century's face of Black male achievement. Yes, Black males would still be exposed to remnants of institutional and systemic discrimination that has in the past crippled their plight. But his election and presence would be a barometer that Black males were embarking upon closing the structural gaps that limited achievement and move toward living in a color-blind society willing to right the discriminatory wrongs of the past. Unfortunately, as stated earlier, since his election to office, the economic and social conditions of the masses of Black males have not improved. Failure in these areas have led national figures such as Smiley and West, and now participants in this book, to be critical of the messages that Obama conveys to Black males.

Obama's constant message has been for Black males to avoid excuses and work through adversity to seize the moment and achieve success as he pleaded to Black male graduates in the 2013 graduation speech at Morehouse College. As mentioned in Chapter Three, this speech that provided an opportunity to address substantive issues facing Black males was met with tremendous backlash. The speech's theme of "no excuses" was filled with criticisms and limited solutions, besides telling future graduates to "stay hungry" and "keep hustling." He spoke to the crowd:

> Sometimes I wrote off my own failings as just another example of the world trying to keep a black man down. I had a tendency sometimes to make excuses for me not doing the right thing. But one of the things that all of you have learned over the last four years is there's no longer any room for excuses.
>
> Well, we've got no time for excuses. Not because the bitter legacy of slavery and segregation have vanished entirely; they have not. Not because racism and discrimination no longer exist; we know those are still out there.[1]

The speech also focused on personal responsibility. He urged graduates to "inspire those who look up to you to expect more of themselves."[2]

But to the contrary, his comments did not address the audience that most desperately needs to hear this message nor the central problems plaguing Black males—economic and social access. Social critics believed his message showed a disconnect with the everyday Black male in the trenches trying to maintain a respectable quality of life, much like his previous lectures on Black fatherhood at the 2008 and 2009 NAACP events. In the commencement speech he embellished the popular view that Black males are to blame for their own shortcomings in the work sector. All with a faulty premise by comparing the struggles of US-born Black males to foreign-born citizens, he declared:

> In today's hyperconnected, hypercompetitive world, with millions of young people from China and India and Brazil—many of whom started with a whole lot less than all of you did—all

of them entering the global workforce alongside you, nobody is going to give you anything that you have not earned.[3]

Obama's main points in the commencement speech were to hold Black males to a standard of individual accountability and personal responsibility—a task he has not undertaken with other communities. As a whole, Black Americans have deemed him the "first Black President" and he has not shied away from the title. However, Obama has on several occasions said he is, "the President of all Americans." In the political realm, Obama has been a "Black president" when it is most advantageous to his reelection. Black vote support in 2008 and 2012 shows the Black communities' loyalty to Obama. When he talks specifically to the Black community, especially Black males, there is discourse created, whether positive or negative. Competing opinions from Black males, and the Black community as a whole, do not negate the influence and depths of his election and presence. It merely indicates that Black males want to have a voice in their evolving social and cultural identity. They look to Obama to foster an economic, social, and political climate that without reservation empowers and uplifts Black males and not to be critical of them in times of need.

The strength of Obama's Blackness is vested in his understanding of the needs and concerns of Black Americans, especially Black males. The implications of his message at Morehouse were that solutions for the social and cultural dysfunctions in the Black male subculture must be addressed by the individual—the Black male—and no excuses are valid. However, he failed to admit that structural origins coupled with limited productive opportunities and quality resources have certainly hindered their economic and social advancement. Indeed, as many participants emphatically stated in interviews, Black males need to get their "shit together" and "do better." They also maintained that realistic societal expectations must be set when there is a dearth of economic and social access. The Morehouse commencement speech shows that even Obama sees the Black male subculture through a prism of bias. While his words were sharp and to the point, the message was dull and did not pierce the psyche of Black males most in need of it.

CONCLUSION

This chapter has presented a set of individual strategies for Black males to carry out in order to increase their probability of triumphing over social circumstances and achieve success. These cultural cues are essential to leading the next generation of young Black males to assume personal responsibility. The dim reality is that society continues to project negative accounts of Black male life. Seldom do we highlight Black males who have achieved personal, academic, and life-long success. American society is primed to view Black males on the basis of stereotypical beliefs that contribute to burdening their plight. But by the accounts of participants in this book, Black males are also huge contributors to the troubles that exist in the Black male subculture. Some Black males have become their own worst enemy—a part of the problem and not the solution.

This discourse began in Chapter One by taking the position that the election and presence of the first Black male president, Barack H. Obama, should have a great influence on reducing the discriminatory perceptions of Black males and increase their personal motivation to achieve success. This was posited under the premise that the historic and symbolic achievement of one man cannot erase the centuries of injustices against the masses of Black males. But his election and presence would boost the level of personal motivation of the Black male subculture. Perhaps the most important questions that now remain are: What is the long-term meaning behind Obama's election? What has truly been his influence on the plight of Black males? And, does his presence define what it means to be a Black male in the twenty-first century? Without question, Obama's election to the presidential office represents the twenty-first century's face of Black male achievement. He embodies the old adage, "You can be anything you set your mind to." An adage that was devoid of the truth until the 2008 Electoral College and popular votes were tallied. Black males are now able to see a model of success in the highest visible office in the United States.

The real challenge, however, is to continue to create an economic, social, and political climate more conducive for Black male success. Equally important is for Black males to adhere to societal expectations by maximizing their given potential and talents and meet the challenges that await. Black males for generations to come will reflect on this period and understand that Obama's election and presence did have an effect on the societal climate. As many participants in this book explained, Obama's impact may have yet to be fully realized. His influence will have a greater impression on the younger generation of Black males.

More than 50 years ago, the Rev. Dr. Martin Luther King Jr. began a crusade to create a social environment to elect the first Black president. That part of King's vision has come to fruition. The election of Obama is not a singular phenomenon. For the sake of future generations, hopefully the legacy of the Obama era will continue to transcend race relations, subvert attached stereotypes, make Black males more culturally progressive, and inspire enormous heights of Black male achievement to witness more "Black boys fly."

I Love Being a Black Man: The Plight, Triumph, and Reflective Mode of Black Male Success

I love being a Black man. I wear my Blackness and masculinity with great pride. As a professional Black man, there have been many trials and tribulation in my quest to achieve personal, academic, and life-long success. Less well known are these stories. My own story is not a singular phenomenon, but it speaks to the depths of what it means to be a Black male in the twenty-first century.

PERSONAL SUCCESS

Today, I am Dr. William T. Hoston. But that is not how my life began. I was born into a dysfunctional family. My father, William L. Hoston, was absent from my life. Like many young Black males, I use to imagine what our lives, my mother and I, would be like if he was a part of it. Instead of choosing to be a part of my life, he choose the latter. The void left by my father's absence had a huge impact on my early social development. I longed for a father to teach me how to ride a bike, shoot the basketball, throw the football, take me to school, help me with homework, come to my graduations, one day be the best man at my wedding, be there for the birth of my children, and be an important part of his grandchildren's lives. What has hurt the most is that my father never attended any of my college graduations—Bachelors (1997), Masters

(1998), and Doctorate (2007). According to a 2010 National Science Foundation (NSF) report on the graduation rate of Black PhDs, in 2007 the year I graduated with my doctorate only 1974 Black Americans in the United States received the degree. Despite our separation over the years, I still invited him and he chose not to attend. This was an accomplishment that a father should share with his son. In the words of the Greek philosopher Plato, "We can easily forgive a child who is afraid of the dark; the real tragedy of life is when men are afraid of the light." Throughout the years, he has been afraid to assume parental responsibility and be a father. His actions left my mother, Janet Smith, to be the sole foundation of my early success. With the help of my mother and other male mentors like my Godfather, Andrew "Sonny" Owens, and adopted brother, Jeffery "Fly" Duffey, I learned over time to channel my energy into positive areas such as sports and education.

Even sadder is that my father has five children with four different women. I have two brothers and two sisters. Both of my younger brothers, Cleveland and Feddrick, are currently in prison. Cleveland is incarcerated for a series of burglary and drug-related crimes. Feddrick is now serving a 25-year prison sentence for voluntary manslaughter and robbery. He killed another Black male for his income tax return check and further contributed to devaluing Black male life. This is the second time he has been in prison. The first time he spent five years in prison for aggravated assault and cruelty to children. Cleveland once wrote in a letter from jail that his life would be different if our father had been there for him growing up. He blamed our father for a lot of things that happened in his life. At an early age, I knew he was on the road most traveled by young Black males. He adopted a criminal lifestyle and that began the revolving door of going in and out of prison.

I tried to have faith over the years that my brothers would see me as a role model and example of success. They each have a strong desire to have the guidance of their father. When a young Black male grows up without a father, someone must fill that void. Personally, my greatest failure in life has been the inability to be the gap between our father's absence and them having the personal motivation to achieve success. Ever since I've dedicated my life to educating and attempting to impact the lives of college students and young people, it is quite troubling that I have not had the same impact on them. Their "Keepin' it Real" and "Education ain't for me" mentality has been detrimental to their personal and life-long success. They adopted these negative philosophies of the Black male subculture. American society labels them as a "drug dealer" and "murder." In my personal world, they are my little brothers. I love them and wouldn't trade them for the world. They both allowed their circumstances to compromise on the choices they made. They needed to have a healthy and stable relationship with our father. The "Educated Big Brother Effect" was not pervasive enough to deter them from falling victim to a street mentality embedded in the Black male subculture. The saying that "some niggas go to college, some niggas go to jail" holds true among some Black males, even in my own family. This reality has brought me to tears on many nights.

The dichotomy of our lives is a microcosm of the strict, no-holds barred nature of my mother. Getting an education was the most important achievement in our household. As much as I loved rap music and sports, she taught me how to value education. For my mother, going to college and receiving a college degree was the only pathway to overcoming personal adversity and achieving long-term success. Even when I stopped playing collegiate football that was a motivating factor in even attending college (as for many young Black males), she reinforced the need to continue and receive a college education. Her sole purpose was to make sure that I graduated from college.

ACADEMIC SUCCESS

In my senior year of high school, I had a difficult time passing the standardized entrance tests to qualify for a football scholarship. I wanted to play college football and eventually make it to the National Football League (NFL). At the time, I believed professional sports were the only avenues of success for Black males. I took the ACT three times and SAT once. The first time I took the ACT I made a 13. The second time I scored a 15. On the third attempt, I made a 17. The NCAA required a 17 on the ACT to qualify for athletic competition. I entered college on a football scholarship at a small school, Nicholls State University (NSU) in Thibodaux, Louisiana. After my first semester in college, I had a 1.93 GPA. I finished the following semester with a 1.5 GPA.

Due to family reasons, I left NSU. Eventually, I landed at the University of New Orleans (UNO). I matriculated from UNO with a bachelors degree in General Studies. My cumulative undergraduate GPA was a 2.93. For the bulk of my undergraduate career, two White men guided my academic success, Drs. Ralph Thayer and Peter Anderson. Both encouraged me to take the Graduate Record Examination (GRE) for graduate school admission. They taught me many valuable lessons on my path to receive the doctorate degree. Yet, there were certain things they could not teach me—how to overcome institutional barriers and gain social acceptance at a predominantly White university. It is difficult at times for White males to gauge the racial climate in such environments oblivious to the privileges their skin color affords them. Therefore, they couldn't provide the soundest advice on the historical racism, stereotypes, and prejudices deeply embedded in the culture of these institutions. I was ultimately able to achieve academic success; however, it was not without hardship and despair. Matriculating on the road to the doctorate degree was a perilous one.

For graduate school, I was accepted to Florida State University (FSU) in the criminology and criminal justice program. At the time, it was the fifth ranked criminology and criminal justice program in the country. In the program, I was met with fundamental racist beliefs. White faculty members questioned the competency of my learning abilities despite showing a firm grasp of the materials. To compound the situation, I didn't "play the game." I was 23 years old, dressed in hip-hop attire, drove a SUV with big rims, played my music loud, never attended program-related event, strongly voiced my opinions in class, and completed the master's degree in one academic year. On one occasion, a professor was giving a lecture on the crack cocaine epidemic in the 1980s, the population most impacted by the drug, and he then put up a PowerPoint on how to make crack cocaine. I proceeded to tell him in so many words that his lecture was disjointed, Whites had flooded the Black community with cocaine and those were not the best ingredients to make crack cocaine. I had just seen a friend of mine make a batch of crack cocaine the prior weekend. In another confrontation, I challenged a professor who said while having a salary of over 100k, he was a proletariat and related to the struggles of Black people. He knew what it felt like to be "Black on the inside." On top of all that, my research focus was on *Gangsta Rap Music and Its Effects on Black Youth*. In 1997, academic research on rap music had not hit its current stride. Needless to say, the word had gotten out among professors that I was an "angry Black man" who liked to challenge the status quo. Honestly, I was not trying to be a nuisance. I was raised in New Orleans, still slightly rough around the edges. I'd never had a talking filter. In retrospect, I simply possessed a robust desire to learn why Black males committed crimes and killed each other. As a consequence of my actions in class and brash presence, I personally witnessed the profound strength of institutional and systemic racism and discrimination.

During the doctorate portion of my graduate studies in 1999, I was met with blatant racial discrimination. After completing course requirements, the next step was to take comprehensive exams. The first time I took the exams, I passed the research methods and statistics section, however failed the criminological theory and criminal justice section by a small margin. Two tenured faculty members on the committee had given me failing marks. Two had scored a high pass and one a low pass. I received a low pass by a non-tenured faculty member. Three votes were needed to pass, however, the two tenured members overruled the committees' decision to pass me. There was no doubt that I was being penalized for speaking out in class against some of the blasphemous comments these two particular professors had made. Five months later on the next round of comprehensive exams, there was a clear fail on the criminological theory and criminal justice section by all members. I left FSU without a doctorate degree. I had obtained a masters and already had a bachelors degree. These degrees were certainly more than what the masses of Black males had achieved. Just four years prior, I was a career undergraduate student, smoking weed and playing video games all day. I left FSU depressed, questioning my academic abilities and believing I had reached the ceiling of my academic achievements.

In 2001, after much soul-searching I resumed my doctoral studies at UNO in political science. I had to rebuild my confidence and listen to the inner voice that said, "Quitting is not an option." I started off slow in the doctorate program. Making all Bs the first few semesters. Soon, I completed coursework and passed comprehensive exams with high honors. Everything seemed to be going as planned until Hurricane Katrina ravaged the city of New Orleans. In late 2005 while working on my dissertation, the storm flooded the city and I was displaced from my home. During this period, I traveled to Atlanta, Georgia, to Dallas, Texas, to Houston, Texas, to Baton Rouge, Louisiana, and back to Houston, Texas, for six months before ultimately settling in Wichita, Kansas, for a few years. I took a visiting assistant professorship position at Wichita State University (WSU) while writing my dissertation. Despite the sum of my social and academic setbacks, I graduated with my doctorate degree in December 2007.

Life-Long Success

As a professional Black man, I've had to battle with conflicting societal expectations from Black and White America in order to sustain life-long success. In Black America, some have viewed me as trying to "act White" in pursuit of my doctorate. Those in the annals of White America have seen me as racially and professionally threatening. Away from work, I can be viewed as a criminal and societal threat to some when walking the streets going about my business. At work, I'm seen at times as a professional threat to Whites (and Blacks) because I maximize my efforts in the work environment to gain appreciation. Yes, I'm a believer of the historical implication that Blacks and minorities in general have to "work twice as hard" to gain success. This bipolar societal perception of professional Black men has great utilities and consequences. Some professional Black men will tell you it was easier to readily be a stagnant member of society unwilling to conform and integrate, never gaining the ability to be indistinguishable from other members in American society—an outlier—a Black Dot. At the end of the day both types of Black men share similar hardships. In some respects, life can be easier this way. When you are a professional Black male, there are heightened societal expectations. Most of all, it takes an adaptive resilient day-to-day approach to be effective under the spotlight of institutional pressures that at times questions your abilities and assumes your position was solely gained through affirmative action.

In these circles, attempting to understand the plight of success for professional Black males is frustrating, but most empathize with each other. The discourse is usually about access, the nonbenefits of White privilege and being judged on potential. These are attributes that propel professional White males. This is also the reason why Black masculinity is always juxtaposed with White masculinity. As we know, Black males are not always afforded the same access. As the old adage goes, "Black folks have to make a way out of no way." This is why when you hear another professional Black male dishonor the symbol, plight, and progress of all Black males it reopens critical dialogue and poses another substantive question: When Black males reach professional success, will American society ever view them differently? Will America judge them based on the content of their character and not the color of their skin? Take, for example, Canadian journalist Orville Lloyd Douglas's 2013 opinion editorial in *The Guardian* titled "Why I Hate Being a Black Man." Douglas was not raised in America; Canada has never had a Black president or an abundance of high-ranking visible Black figures to elicit the hope of a better America for Black males. He believes the color of his skin is a "personal prison" and the cultural phrase born in the 1960s that "black is beautiful" simply is not true. He explains in the piece:

> I can honestly say I hate being a black male. Although black people like to wax poetic about loving their label I hate "being black." I just don't fit into a neat category of the stereotypical views people have of black men. In popular culture, black men are recognized in three areas: sports, crime, and entertainment. I hate rap music, I hate most sports.[1]

Despite his success as a college-educated journalist, Douglas believes that White society still sees him as "a six-foot tall black man with broad shoulders" and "dark skin, broad nose, large thick lips." The inability to escape the negative cultural view of his dark Black skin despite his personal and academic accomplishments has led to self-hate. He personally believes, "There is nothing special or wonderful about being a black male—it is a life of misery and shame."[2] The internal and external self-hate posed in the piece exhibits his disdain for the limited scope of Blackness and Black masculinity. A part of me understands his frustration with being a professional Black male that is still seen in some social environments as a "thug," "criminal," or "nigger." The openness of his opinion editorial should be applauded. Greater awareness makes you have a strong disdain for the judgmental nature of White society. Then you further understand that even if you are an honest, hardworking Black male or have an advanced degree (e.g., JD, PhD, MD) certain segments of White society, in the United States, Canada, or globally, will still see you as and consider you to be a "nigger." This is the sad truth.

I compare the personal sentiments of Douglas to my own life's journey as a professional Black male because at times I've had similar thoughts. While I've never questioned my self-worth with regard to the Black male subculture, I have strongly questioned the hardship, struggle, emotional stress, White hazing, reluctant conformity, and constant institutional pressures to be better than my White male counterparts worth obtaining a doctorate degree when certain segments devalue my plight and view me in negative terms. Once you actually overcome the structural and cultural forces that have targeted Black males, you are still compared to the mass pool—an outlier—a Black Dot.

The foresight of my life-long success is a continuum. On the days I feel like Douglas, I summon the spirits of Kunta Kinte, Nat Turner, W. E. B. DuBois, Huey Newton, Dr. Rev. Martin Luther King Jr., and El-Hajj Malik El-Shabazz to give me strength. Life doesn't get easier for Black males; we have to continue to be resilient. The main difference between Douglas and myself is that in spite of White America's skewed perspective on Black male life, I am comfortable in my Black skin and wholeheartedly accept there will never be full racial acceptance and equality in my lifetime. The trials in my life shaped me to love my being as a Black male. His trials unfortunately have eroded his self-identity and created a feeling of self-hatred. Orville Lloyd Douglas is not the first professional Black male to hate being a Black man (and won't be the last). The conflict of double-consciousness is still alive and well. One of the outcomes of being a professional Black male in American society is to understand you are one of the few. Black male achievement can come with a heavy burden and responsibility to be strong in order to help uplift and empower other Black males.

Appendix A.1: Interview Schedule of Black Male Participants

The interviews of Black males were conducted between March 27, 2009, and July 17, 2013. A purposeful sample of participants was chosen from Wichita, Kansas; Houston, Texas; New Orleans, Louisiana; Washington, DC; and Atlanta, Georgia. This project was partially funded by the University of Houston—Clear Lake, via the Faculty Research and Support Fund (FRSF_2010).

The research team was composed of university students and myself. We solicited interviews face-to-face, by phone, email, and via online through surveymonkey.com. The majority of Black males were interviewed face-to-face using semistructured, open-ended questions. As described by Berg (1998, 61), "this type of interview involves the implementation of a number of predetermined questions…in a systematic and consistent order, but the interviewers are allowed freedom to digress; that is, the interviewers are permitted to probe far beyond the answers." All face-to-face and phone interviews averaged around 20–35 minutes in length. The length of the interviews varied depending on the depth of the responses. Each respondent was asked the same series of questions from the interview schedule. In some cases responses were too narrow and needed follow-up questions for further clarification. Beamer (2002, 92) indicates that the researcher should ask more broad questions at the beginning of the interview to allow the respondent to speak freely and follow-up with more specific questions. He suggests that this approach permits the interview to stay more structured and focused. Once each interview was complete, each audiotape was transcribed and reviewed.

Professional and ethical standards were adhered to in maintaining the confidentiality of the information provided. This research used pseudonyms for participants. The anonymity of research participants was maintained to allow full disclosure on questions and their position on topics discussed in the book. The responses were treated confidentially. In social science research it is important for participants to know that their responses if published will not be identifiable as theirs (Robson 1995, 43). The demographics of occupation and age were current at the time of this writing.

The final number of Black males interviewed in each city is as follows: Wichita, Kansas—31; Houston, Texas—58; New Orleans, Louisiana—39; Washington, DC —22; Atlanta, Georgia—35. A total of 185 Black males were interviewed.

QUESTION WORDING

Evaluation of Black Male Identity

1. What does it mean to be a Black male in the twenty-first century?

Black Linked Fate

2. Do you think that what happens generally to Black people in this country will have something to do with what happens in your life?

Influence of Rap Music

3. What are your thoughts on the current state of rap music?
4. How has rap music influenced Black males?

Crime

5. Would you say that the amount of crime in (your city) has increased, decreased, or remained about the same over the last several years?
6. Do you think it is warranted for Black males to be perceived as violent criminals?
7. What is your opinion on Black-on-Black murders?

Employment

8. When Black people are not getting jobs, is it the government in Washington's responsibility or the individual's responsibility to obtain employment?

Education

9. How would you rate the quality of public education in (your city)?
10. Do you think there is a still a gap in academic achievement among Black and White youth?

Vote Choice

11. Who did you vote for in the presidential election, November 4th 2008?
12. Who did you vote for in the presidential election, November 6th 2012?

Black Solidarity

13. How important is it for Blacks to vote for Black candidates when they run for office?

Obama Effect

14. Would you say that the election and presence of President Barack H. Obama, as the first Black president, has motivated you to work harder or about the same to achieve success?

Symbolic Racism

15. Over the past few years, have Blacks gotten more or less than they deserve with President Barack H. Obama in office?

Self-Improvement

16. In general, what is the best advice you can give to Black males to achieve success?

Appendix A.2: Chapter Two Methodology

PARTICIPANTS

Students volunteered to participate in the study from three political science courses and four sociology courses over the fall 2008 and spring 2009 semesters. Data were pooled from two consecutive semesters. A baseline survey was administered to a convenient sample of Black undergraduate students at a Midwestern University to determine whether or not rap songs that contain the misogynistic message of sexual assault and rape shaped their attitudes. There were two groups, an experimental group and control group. In the experimental group, there were 83 students. There were 53 males (64 percent) and 30 females (36 percent). The mean age was (21.2). The control group contained 61 students. There were 26 males (43 percent) and 35 females (57 percent). All participants ranged in academic year from freshman to senior. The mean age was (20.8).

PROCEDURE

The study received approval from the Institutional Review Board. Those that participated were told that the purpose of the study was to gauge the current state of rap music and whether artists should be more accountable for their lyrical content (see Chapter Two for full description of *Procedure*).

INSTRUMENTATION

Participants were asked to complete a 14-question survey. They were asked their age, gender, academic classification, and various questions related to rap music and misogyny. Questions were constructed on a Likert scale. This type of scale measures whether participants have either positive or negative responses to a statement. After completion of the survey, the participants' responses were summed to create a score for each question item. The survey questions are as follows:

QUESTIONS

1. What is your age?
2. What is your gender?
3. What is your academic classification?
4. How often do you listen to rap music?
   Response categories: 5. Very Frequent (20+ hours a week); 4. Frequent (12–19 hours a week); 3. Sometimes (6–11 hours a week); 2. Rarely (1–5 hours a week); 1. Never (0 hours a week).
5. What do you pay attention to most when listening to rap music?
   Response categories: The instrumental beat, The lyrical content, Both equally.
6. In general, would you classify your attitude toward rap music as:
   Response categories: Positive, Neutral, Negative.
7. Do you believe that rap songs are more offensive to males or females or both? Response categories: Males, Females, Both equally.
8. Which misogynistic message do you find most offensive in rap music?
   Response categories:
   a. Derogatory name-calling.
   b. Prostitution and pimping.
   c. Legitimation of physical violence against females.
   d. Sexual assault and rape.
   e. None of the above.
9. Do you believe that rap music provokes disrespectful attitudes toward females? Response categories: 5. Strongly agree; 4. Somewhat agree; 3. Neutral; 2. Somewhat disagree; 1. Strongly disagree.

10. Do you believe that rap music promotes aggressive and violent behavior toward females? Response categories: 5. Strongly agree; 4. Somewhat agree; 3. Neutral; 2. Somewhat disagree; 1. Strongly disagree.

11. Do you believe that rap music encourages the sexual assault and rape of females? Response categories: 5. Strongly agree; 4. Somewhat agree; 3. Neutral; 2. Somewhat disagree; 1. Strongly disagree.

12. Do you believe that rap music shapes male listeners' attitudes toward sexually assaulting and raping females? Response categories: 5. Strongly agree; 4. Somewhat agree; 3. Neutral; 2. Somewhat disagree; 1. Strongly disagree.

13. Do you believe that rap artists should be more accountable for their lyrical content? Response categories: 5. Strongly agree; 4. Somewhat agree; 3. Neutral; 2. Somewhat disagree; 1. Strongly disagree.

14. What are your thoughts on the current state of rap music?

Limitations

There were several limitations of the survey. First, the sample may not be generalizable to other Black college students, Blacks living in the Midwest, or the mass Black population. Second, the Likert scale only measures agreement or disagreement with a statement. There was no narrative for each individual response. Third, as with all surveys, it is impossible to know whether participants were truthful with their answers.

NOTES

INTRODUCTION

1. See the opinion editorial, "A Poverty of the Mind," by Orlando Patterson, March 26, 2006, *The New York Times*, Available at http://www.nytimes.com/2006/03/26/opinion /26patterson.html.

1 THE BLACK MALE IDENTITY

1. See the opinion editorial, "What Obama isn't: Black like me on race," by Stanley Crouch, November 2, 2006, *New York Daily News*. Available at http://www.nydailynews.com /archives/opinions/obama-isn-black-race-article-1.585922.
2. Ibid.
3. See the opinion editorial, "Colorblind: Barack Obama would be the great black hope in the next president race—if he were actually black," by Debra J. Dickerson, January 22, 2007, *Salon*. Available at http://www.salon.com/2007/01/22 /obama_161.
4. Transcript from the interview, "No bias no bull: Race in the Race: The great unknown," by Charlie Rose, October 11, 2008, *CNN*. Available at http://transcripts.cnn.com /TRANSCRIPTS/0810/11/se.03.html.
5. The Father's Day speech by Sen. Barack Obama (D-Ill.) to the Apostolic Church of God in Chicago, Illinois was on June 15, 2008. Transcript of speech available at http://www.politico .com/news/stories/0608/11094.html.
6. In 1858, Senator Stephen A. Douglas and Abraham Lincoln faced each other in a series of seven debates for the Illinois Senator seat. One of the many questions asked was whether slavery should be extended to the territories. On September 18, 1858, Lincoln made this statement. See R. P. Basler. 1953. *Collected works of Abraham Lincoln*. New Brunswick, NJ: Rutgers University Press, Volume 3:145–146.

7. See Wilson, pages 5–23 for an in-depth analysis of structural and cultural factors. For a thorough review on cultural factors that impact Black males, see Orlando Patterson, "Taking Culture Seriously: A Framework and an Afro-American Illustration," in *Culture matters: How values shape human progress*, ed. L. E. Harrison and S. P. Huntington (New York: Basic Books, 2000), p. 202–218. Also, in Chapter Three, I will provide a detailed account of how these structural and cultural factors impact Black males in a case study of Black-on-Black murders in Chicago, Illinois.

8. US Department of Labor, Bureau of Labor Statistics (http://www.bls.gov/cps/).

9. See the report by Bruce Western and Becky Pettit, 2009. Available at http://www.pewtrusts.org/uploadedFiles/wwwpewtrustsorg/Reports/Economic_Mobility/Collateral%20Costs%20FINAL.pdf.

10. This chart does not include the count from studio songs with the rap group Hot Boyz (1996–2001), mixtapes with rap group The Sqad (1999–2003), his duo album with Birdman titled *Like Father, Like Son* (2006), solo mixtapes, or song features. Lil Wayne's usage of the N-word is much more excessive in his mixtapes.

2 WE ALL CAME FROM A WOMAN: RAP MUSIC AND MISOGYNY

1. See the article "Rick Ross Issues Official Apology for 'Rape' Lyrics," by R. J. Cubarrubia, April 12, 2013, *Rolling Stone*. Available at http://www.rollingstone.com/music/news/rick-ross-apologizes-for-pro-rape-lyrics-20130412.

2. See 2011 UCR, Tables 43, A-C; Available at http://www.fbi.gov/about-us/cjis/ucr/crime-in-the-u.s/2011/crime-in-the-u.s.-2011/tables/table-43; One of the difficulties in understanding the relationship between race and crime is the failure of the UCR to distinguish between Hispanics and whites. The UCR combines most Hispanics in the "White" category.

3. See the NCVS report, "Criminal Victimization, 2012," authored by Jennifer Truman, Lynn Langton, and Michael Planty, October 2013. Available at http://www.bjs.gov/content/pub/pdf/cv12.pdf.

4. See the NCVS report, "Criminal Victimization, 2010," authored by Jennifer Truman, September 2011. Available at http://www.bjs.gov/content/pub/pdf/cv10.pdf.

3   BLACK-ON-BLACK MURDERS: A CASE STUDY OF CHIRAQ, KILLINOIS

1. See CPD Murder Analysis Report for White victims: 2011 (5 percent); 2010 (4 percent); 2009 (3 percent); 2008 (6 percent); 2007 (6 percent); 2006 (6 percent); 2005 (6 percent); 2004 (7 percent); 2003 (7 percent).

2. See CPD Murder Analysis Report for White offenders: 2011 (4 percent); 2010 (5 percent); 2009 (4 percent); 2008 (4 percent); 2007 (4 percent); 2006 (4 percent); 2005 (5 percent); 2004 (5 percent); 2003 (4 percent).

3. *Huffington Post Chicago.* (2012, June 16). "Chicago Homicides Outnumber U.S. Troop Killings In Afghanistan." Available at http://www.huffingtonpost.com/2012/06/16/chicago -homicide-rate-wor_n_1602692.html.

4. Chapter Four provides a full discussion on race and representation for Black Americans.

5. See C. Newman, 2012. "Obama Talks Chicago Violence and Murders with MTV News." *Chicago Sun-Times.* Available at http://blogs.suntimes.com/politics/2012/10/obama_talks _chicago_violence_with_mtv.html (October 29).

6. In the case of *McDonald* v. *Chicago*, No. 08–1521, the U.S. Supreme Court in a 5–4 vote overturned state and local laws in Illinois that banned handgun possession.

7. Excerpt from July 13, 2013, news conference. See *ABC local news*, "CPD Supt. Garry McCarthy Calls for Tougher Gun, Sentencing Laws." Available at http://abclocal.go.com/wls /story?section=news/local&id=9189098.

8. "President Obama Makes a Statement on the Shooting in Newtown, Connecticut," *The White House*, December 14, 2012, www.whitehouse.gov/photos-and-video/video/2012 /12/14/president-obama-makes-statement-shooting -newtown-connecticut.

9. A full description of the 23 Executive Orders can be found at the White House official website: http://www.whitehouse .gov/sites/default/files/docs/wh_now_is_the_time_full.pdf.

10. The roll-call breakdown in the first round of concealed carry voting, Senate 45–12 and House 89–28; The full text of both versions, HB1453 and HB183, of the *Firearm Concealed Carry Act* are available at the Illinois General Assembly website: http://www.ilga.gov. At the time of these votes 32 Black legislators occupied seats of the 177 total members in the 98th Illinois General Assembly. There were 11 Senate members and

21 House members. Proportionally, Black legislators represent 19 percent of the legislative body in the Senate (59), 18 percent in the House (118), and 18 percent overall (177).

11. J. O'Connor, 2013. "Illinois Concealed Carry: House Passes Bill That Could End State's Long-Running Ban On Firearms." *Huffington Post.* Available at http://www.huffingtonpost .com/2013/05/31/illinois-concealed-carry-_9_n_3368691 .html (May 31).

12. The full text of HB 1189, *Gun Safety and Responsibility Act* is available at the Illinois General Assembly website: http:// www.ilga.gov.

13. See the Illinois state police website for the criteria to obtain a firearm owners identification (FOID) card. Available at http:// www.isp.state.il.us/foid/foidinfo.cfm.

14. See the July 17, 2013, press release, "City Council Passes Ordinance to Protect Students from Gun Violence." Available at http://www.cityofchicago.org/content/dam/city /depts/mayor/Press%20Room/Press%20Releases/2013 /July/7.17.13safetyzone.pdf.

15. See the report, "From High School to the Future: The Challenge of Senior Year in Chicago Public Schools," authored by Melissa Roderick, Vanessa Coca, Eliza Moeller, and Thomas Kelley-Kemple, February 2013. Available at https://ccsr.uchicago .edu/sites/default/files/publications/Senior%20Year%20 -%20Final.pdf.

16. For more information on "The Reauthorization of the Elementary and Secondary Education Act," see the *U.S. Department of Education* website, March 2010. Document available at http://www2.ed.gov/policy/elsec/leg/blueprint /blueprint.pdf.

17. "Helping America Become a 'Grad Nation,'" *The White House*, March 1, 2010, http://www.whitehouse.gov/photos-and -video/video/helping-america-become-a-grad-nation.

18. See the article, "Phaseout Plan Pains Chicago Neighborhood," by Jaclyn Zubrzycki, October 17, 2012, *Education Week.* Available at http://ew.edweek.org/nxtbooks/epe /ew_10172012/index.php?startid=12.

19. For more information on the *Safe Passage* program, see the CPS website. Information available at http://www.cps.edu /Programs/Wellness_and_transportation /Safetyandsecurity/safepassage/Pages/Safepassage.aspx.

20. See the Illinois Department of Employment Security, Economic Information and Analysis: http://www.ides.illinois .gov/page.aspx?item=2509; Also see, "Black Metropolitan Unemployment in 2011," by Algernon Austin, July 2, 2012, *Economic Policy Institute*. Available at http://www.epi.org /files/2013/ib337-black-metropolitan-unemployment.pdf.

21. "The Depression in the Teen Labor Market in Illinois in Recent Years," *Center for Labor Market Studies*, January 2012 Northeastern University. Available at http://www.northeastern .edu/clms/wp-content/uploads/The-Depression-in-the -Teen-Labor-Market-in-the-State-of-Illinois-in-Recent-Years -1-12-12.pdf.

22. Morehouse College is the only all-male historically Black college in the United States.

23. For the full transcript of the graduate speech, see "Prepared text for President Obama's speech at Morehouse," *The Atlanta Journal-Constitution*. Available at http://www.ajc.com/news /news/local/prepared-text-for-president-obamas-speech-at -moreh/nXwk2/ (May 19, 2013).

4   LIVING IN THE OBAMA ERA

1. For the full transcript of Obama's 2012 victory speech, see "Audio and Transcript: Obama's Victory Speech," *NPR*. Available at http://www.npr.org/2012/11/06/164540079 /transcript-president-obamas-victory-speech (November 7, 2012).

2. For the full transcript of Obama's 2004 DNC speech, see "Transcript: Illinois Senate Candidate Barack Obama," *The Washington Post*. Available at http:// www. washingtonpost .com/wp-dyn/articles/A19751–2004Jul27.html (July 27, 2004).

3. See the opinion editorial, "Profiling Obama," by Bill Keller, July 28, 2013, *The New York Times*, Available at http://www .nytimes.com/2013/07/29/opinion/keller-profiling-obama .html.

4. See the article, "Study: Non-Voting Felons Increasing," by Staff, September 21, 2013, *ABC News*, Available at http://abcnews .go.com/Politics/story?id=121724.

5. Ibid.

6. Ibid.

7. For the full transcript of Obama addressing the *Race to the Top* program, see "President Obama on Education: 'The Status Quo Is Morally Inexcusable,'" *The White House*. Available at http://www.whitehouse.gov/blog/2010/07/29/president-obama-education-status-quo-morally-inexcusable (July 29, 2010).

8. US Sentencing Commission. 2009. *Annual Report*. Washington, DC: U.S. Sentencing Commission. Available at http://www.ussc.gov/Research_and_ Statistics/Annual_Reports_and_Sourcebooks/2009/ar09toc.htm.

9. For the full transcript, see Senator Barack Obama, "Remarks at Howard University Convocation," September 28, 2007. Available at http://www.barackobama.com/2007/09/28/remarks_of_senator_barack_obam_26.php.

10. See the article, "Ben Carson: Obamacare Worst Thing to Happen to the U.S. Since Slavery." By Cheryl Wetzstein, *The Washington Times*. October 11, 2013. Available at http://m.washingtontimes.com/news/2013/oct/11/ben-carson-obamacare-worst-thing-slavery/.

11. See the report, "King's Dream Remains an Elusive Goal: Many Americans See Racial Disparities." *Pew Research Center*, August 22, 2013. Available at http://www.pewsocialtrends.org/files/2013/08/final_full_report_racial_disparities.pdf.

12. See the recorded interview and obtain transcript at the *Democracy Now!* website, November 9, 2012. Available at http://www.democracynow.org/2012/11/9/tavis_smiley_cornel_west_on_the

13. See the recorded interview at BET.com, November 8, 2012. Available at http://www.bet.com/shows/dont-sleep/sleep-talkers/2012/11/marc-lamont-hill-chris-pena-sandra-guzman.html.

5   Black Boy Fly

1. For the full transcript of the graduate speech, see "Prepared Text for President Obama's Speech at Morehouse," *The Atlanta Journal-Constitution*. Available at http://www.ajc.com/news/news/local/prepared-text-for-president-obamas-speech-at-moreh/nXwk2/ (May 19, 2013).

2. Ibid.

3. Ibid.

Postscript I Love Being a Black Man: The Plight, Triumph, and Reflective Mode of Black Male Success

1. See the article, "Why I Hate Being a Black Man," by Orville Lloyd Douglas, November 9, 2013, *The Guardian*. Available at http://www.theguardian.com/commentisfree/2013/nov /09/i-hate-being-a-black-man.
2. Ibid.

References

Adams, T. M., and D. B. Fuller. 2006. The words have changed but the ideology remains the same: Misogynistic lyrics in rap music. *Journal of Black Studies* 36(6): 938–957.

Alexander, M. 2010. *The new Jim Crow: Mass incarceration in the age of colorblindness.* New York: The New Press.

Anderson, E. 1997. The precarious balance: Race man or sellout? In Ellis Cose (Ed.), *The Darden dilemma* (114–132). New York: Harper Perennial.

Anderson, E. 1999. *Code of the streets: Decency, violence, and the moral life of the inner city.* New York: W. W. Norton & Company, Inc.

Armstrong, E. G. 2001. Gangsta misogyny: A content analysis of the portrayals of violence against women in rap music, 1987–1993. *Journal of Criminal Justice and Popular Culture* 8(2): 96–126.

Aronson, J., Jannone, S., McGlone, M., and T. Johnson-Campbell. 2009. The Obama effect: An experimental test. *Journal of Experimental Social Psychology* 45(4): 957–960.

Asante, M. K. 2000. *The Egyptian philosophers: Ancient African voices from Imhotep to Akhenaten.* Chicago: African American Images.

Barongan, C., and G. C. Hall-Nagayama. 1995. The influence of misogynous rap music on sexual aggression against women. *Psychology of Women Quarterly* 19(2): 195–207.

Beamer, G. 2002. Elite interviews and state politics research. *State Politics and Policy Quarterly* 2(1): 86–96.

Berg, B. L. 1998. *Qualitative research methods for the social sciences* (3rd edn.). Boston: Allyn and Bacon.

Bergner, G. 1998. Myths of the masculinity subject: Freud's Oedipus complex and Douglass's 1845 narrative. In C. Lane (Ed.), *The psychoanalysis of race* (241–260). New York: Columbia University Press.

Berry, V. T., and H. Looney. 1996. Rap music, Black men, and the police. In V. T. Berry and C. Manning-Miller (Eds.), *Mediated message and African-American culture* (263–277). Thousand Oaks, CA: Sage.

Bond, J. R., and R. Fleisher. 1990. *The president in the legislative arena*. Chicago:University of Chicago Press.

Boyd, H. 2007. It's hard out here for a Black man! *The Black Scholar* 37(3): 2–9.

Burnside, R., and K. Whitehurst. 2007. From the statehouse to the White House? Barack Obama's bid to become the next president. *Journal of Black Studies* 38(1): 75–89.

Canon, D. T. 1999. *Race, redistricting, and representation: The unintended consequences of Black majority districts*. Chicago: University of ChicagoPress.

Cobb, M. D., and W. A. Boettcher. 2007. Ambivalent sexism and misogynistic rap music: Does exposure to Eminem increase sexism? *Journal of Applied Social Psychology* 37(12): 3025–3042.

Cureton, S. R. 2009. Something wicked this way comes: A historical account of Black gangsterism offers wisdom and warning for African American leadership. *Journal of Black Studies* 40(2): 347–361.

Davis, A. Y. 1993. Billie Holiday's "strange fruit": Music and social consciousness. In Gerald Early (Vol. 2, Ed.), *Speech and power: The African American essay and its cultural content from polemics to pulpit*. (33–43). Hopewell, NJ: Ecco Press.

Davis, L. E., Ajzen, I., Saunders, J., and T. Williams. 2002. The decision of African American students to complete high school: An application of the theory of planned behavior. *Journal of Educational Psychology* 94(4): 810–819.

Dawson, M. C. 1994. *Behind the mule: Race and class in African-American politics*.Princeton: Princeton University Press.

Douglass, F. 1970. *My bondage and my freedom*. Chicago: Johnson Publishing Company.

DuBois, W. E. B. 1903. *The souls of Black folk*. New York: Bantam Classic.

Edwards, G. C. III. 1980. *Presidential influence in Congress*. San Francisco: W. H. Freeman.

Ellison, R. 1952. *Invisible man*. New York: Random House.

Friedman, J. 1994. *Cultural identity and global process*. London, UK: Sage.

George, N. 1998. *Hip hop America*. New York: Penguin Press.

Goldman, S. K. 2010. *Effects of the 2008 Obama presidential campaign on White racial prejudice*. Unpublished doctoral dissertation. University of Pennsylvania, Philadelphia, PA.

Gourdine, R. M., and B. P. Lemmons. 2011. Perceptions of misogyny in hip hop and rap: What do the youths think? *Journal of Human Behavior in the Social Environment* 21(1): 57–72.

Gray, V. 2013. *The impact of the American recovery and reinvestment act of 2009 on Black and Latino unemployment.* Unpublished doctoral dissertation. Clark Atlanta University, Atlanta, GA.

Hall-Nagayama, G. C., and R. Hirschman. 1991. Toward a theory of sexual aggression: A quadripartite model. *Journal of Consulting and Clinical Psychology* 59(5): 662–669.

Haney-Lopez, I. F. 1994. Social construction of race: Some observations on illusion, fabrication, and choice. *The Harvard Civil Rights-Civil Liberties Law Review* 29(1): 1–62.

Hansen, C. H. 1995. Predicting cognitive and behavioral effects of gangsta rap. *Basic and Applied Social Psychology* 16(1–2): 43–52.

Hassan-El, K. M. 1999. *The Willie Lynch letter and the making of a slave.* Chicago: Frontline Distribution International.

Haynie, K. L. 2001. *African-American legislators in the American states.* New York: Columbia University Press.

Herring, M. 1990. Legislative responsiveness to Black constituents in three Deep South states. *Journal of Politics* 52(3): 740–758.

hooks, b. 2004. *We real cool. Black men and masculinity.* New York: Routledge.

Horton, A. 2009. Violence against the young: The new urban challenges. *Journal of Human Behavior in the Social Environment* 19(7): 885–901.

Hughes, L. A., and J. F. Short Jr. 2005. Disputes involving youth street gang members: Micro-Social contexts. *Criminology* 43(1): 43–76.

Hunter, A. G., and J. E. Davis. 1994. Hidden voices of Black men: The meaning, structure, and complexity of manhood. *Journal of Black Studies* 25(1): 20–40.

Johnson, J. D., Adams, M. S., Ashburn, L., and W. Reed. 1995. Differential gender effects of exposure to rap music on African American adolescents' acceptance of teen dating violence. *Sex Roles* 33(7–8): 597–605.

Johnson, J. D., Jackson, L. A., and L. Gatto. 1995. Violent attitudes and deferred academic aspirations: Deleterious effects of exposure to rap music. *Basic and Applied Social Psychology* 16(1–2): 27–41.

Jenkins, T. S. 2006. Mr. Nigger: The challenges of educating Black males within American society. *Journal of Black Studies* 37(1): 127–155.

Kelley, R. D. G. 1994. *Race rebels: Culture, politics, and the Black working class.* New York: Free Press.

Kennedy, R. 2002. *Nigger: The strange career of a troublesome word.* New York: Vintage Books.

Kitwana, B. 2002. *The hip-hop generation: Young Blacks and the crisis in African American culture.* New York: Basic Books.

Klein, G. C. 2008. For the new commander in chief: A violence prevention strategy. *Journal of Police Crisis Negotiations* 9(1): 55–60.

Kreider, R. M., and R. Ellis. 2011. "Living arrangements of children: 2009," *Current Population Reports*, pp. 70–126, US Census Bureau, Washington, DC. Available at http://www.census.gov/prod/2011pubs/p70-126.pdf.

LaFree, G. D. 1982. Male power and female victimization: Toward a theory of interracial rape. *American Journal of Sociology* 88(2): 311–328.

Laseter, R. L. 1997. The labor force participation of young Black men: A qualitative examination. *Social Service Review* 71(1): 72–88.

Lipman, P. 2002. Making the global city, making inequality: The political economy and cultural politics of Chicago school policy. *American Educational Research Journal* 39(2): 379–419.

Locke, A. 1925. *The new Negro: An interpretation.* New York: A. & C. Boni.

Lopez, M. H., and P. Taylor. 2009. "Dissecting the 2008 electorate: Most diverse in U.S. history." Washington, DC: Pew Research Center. Available at http://pewhispanic.org/files/reports/108.pdf (April 30).

Mansbridge, J. 1999. Should Blacks represent Blacks and women represent women? A contingent "yes." *Journal of Politics* 61(3): 628–657.

Martin, T. S. 1972. Inequality in desegregation: Black school closings. *The University of Chicago Law Review* 39(3): 658–672.

Marx, D. M., Ko, S. J., and R. A. Friedman. 2009. The "Obama effect": How a salient role model reduces race-based performance differences. *Journal of Experimental Social Psychology* 45(4): 953–956.

McCormick, J. P., and C. E. Jones. 1993. The conceptualization of deracialization. In Georgia Persons (Ed.), *Dilemmas of Black politics* (66–84). New York: Harper Collins.

Miller, C. M. 1990. Agenda-Setting by state legislative Black caucuses: Policy priorities and factors of success. *Policy Studies Review* 9(2): 339–354.

Nelson, A. J. 1991. *Emerging influentials in state legislatures: Women, Black, and Hispanics.* New York: Praeger.

Nunn, R. L. 2005. Lock them up and throw away the vote. *Chicago Journal of International Law* 5(2): 763–783.

Obama, B. 1995. *Dreams from my father: A story of race and inheritance*. New York:Crown Publishers.

Obama, B. 2006. *The audacity of hope: Thoughts on reclaiming the American dream*. New York: Crown Publishers.

Ogbar, J. O. G. 2007. *Hip-Hop revolution: The culture and politics of rap*. Kansas: University of Kansas Press.

Perry, H. L. 1990. Recent advances in Black electoral politics. *PS: Political Science and Politics* 23(2): 141–142.

Perry, H. L. 1996. Introduction: An analysis of major themes in the concept of deracialization. In Huey L. Perry (Ed.), *Race, politics, and governance in the United States* (1–11). Gainesville: University Press of Florida.

Pitkin, H. F. 1967. *The concept of representation*. University of California Press.

Reiman, J., and P. Leighton. 2013. *The rich get richer and the poor get prison: Ideology, class, and criminal justice* (10th edn.). Upper Saddle River, NJ: Pearson.

Robson, C. 1995. *Real world research*. Oxford: Blackwell.

Rose, T. 1994. *Black noise: Rap music and Black culture in contemporary America*. Hanover, NH: Wesleyan University Press.

Rudman, L. A., and M. R. Lee. 2002. Implicit and explicit consequences of exposure toviolent and misogynous rap music. *Group Processes and Intergroup Relations* 5(2): 133–150.

Sander, W. 1985. Economic aspects of single parenthood in Chicago. *Journal of Marriage and Family* 47(2): 497–502.

Sargent, J. 1991. "Black interest and representation." Paper presented at the annual meeting of the American Political Science Association, Washington, DC.

Smith, K. C. 2011. *The Obama effect on African-American students' academicperformance*. Unpublished doctoral dissertation. Howard University, Washington, DC.

Smith, S. L. 2005. From Dr. Dre to dismissed: Assessing violence, sex, and substance use on MTV. *Critical Studies in Media Communications* 22(1): 89–98.

South, S. J., and R. B. Felson. 1990. The racial patterning of rape. *Social Forces* 69(1): 71–93.

Swain, C. M. 1993. *Black faces, Black interests: The representation of African Americans in Congress*. Cambridge: Harvard University Press.

Took, K., and D. S. Weiss. 1994. The relationship between heavy metal and rap music and adolescent turmoil: Real or artifact. *Adolescence* 29(115): 613–621.

US Bureau of the Census: *Statistical abstract of the U.S. 2010*: U.S. Census, Washington, DC 2010.

US Bureau of the Census: *2007–2011 American Community Survey*: U.S. Census, Washington, DC 2011.

Wade, B. H., and C. A. Thomas-Gunnar. 1993. Explicit rap music lyrics and attitudes toward rape: The perceived effects on African American college students' attitudes. *Challenge: A Journal of Research on African American Men* 4(1): 51–60.

Walters, R. 2007. Barack Obama and the politics of Blackness. *Journal of Black Studies* 38(1): 7–29.

Walton, H. Jr. 1985. *Invisible politics: Black political behavior.* Albany: State University of New York Press.

Weitzer, R., and C. E. Kubrin. 2009. Misogyny in rap music: A content analysis of prevalence and meanings. *Men and Masculinities* 12(1): 3–29.

Welch, S., and L. Sigelman. 2011. The "Obama effect" and White racial attitudes. *The ANNALS of the American Academy of Political and Social Science* 634(1): 207–220.

Wilson, W. J. 1996. *When work disappears: The world of the new urban poor.* New York: Vintage Books.

Woldemikael, T. 1989. A case study of race consciousness among Haitian immigrants. *Journal of Black Studies* 20(2): 224–239.

Wyatt, G. E. 1992. The sociocultural contest of African American and White American women's rape. *Journal of Social Issues* 48(1): 77–91.

Yancey, D. 1988. *When hell froze over.* Roanoke, VA: Taylor Publishing Company.

DISCOGRAPHY

Big L, "Devil's Son" in *Return of the Devil's Son* (CD; Flamboyant Music Group, 2010).

Big L, "Harlem Nights" in *L Corleone* (CD; Flamboyant Music Group, 2012).

B.O.N.E. Enterpri$e aka Bone Thugs-n-Harmony, "Def Dick" in *Faces of Death* (CD; Stoney Burke Records, 1993).

Dead Prez, "They" Schools," in *Let's Get Free* (CD; Columbia Records, 2000).

DMX, "X Is Coming" in *It's Dark and Hell Is Hot* (CD; Ruff Ryders, Def Jam, 1998).

Freddie Gibbs, "187 Proof" in *Cold Day in Hell* (CD; Corporate Thugz, 2011).

Geto Boys, "Mind of a Lunatic" in *Grip It! On That Other Level* (CD; Rap-A-Lot Records, 1989).

Hopsin, "Ill Mind of Hopsin 5" (Single; Funk Volume/Hopsin, 2012).

Kayne West and Jay-Z, "Murder to Excellence" in *Watch the Trone* (CD; Roc-A-Fella, Roc Nation, Def Jam, 2011).

Kendrick Lamar, "Black Boy Fly" in *Good Kid, M.A.A.D City* (CD; Aftermath Entertainment, Interscope Records, 2012)

Lauryn Hill, "Superstar" in *The Miseducation of Lauryn Hill* (CD; Ruffhouse, Columbia Records, 1998),

Nelly, "Tip Drill" in *Da Derrty Versions: The Reinvention* (CD; Derrty Enterprises, 2003).

N.O.R.E.,"Scared Money" from unreleased album *S.U.P.E.R.T.H.U.G.* (CD; Conglomerate Records, 2011).

Notorious B.I.G., "Just Playing (Dreams)" in *Ready to Die The Remaster* (CD; Bad Boy Records, 1994).

Notorious B.I.G., "What's Beef?" in *Life After Death* (CD; Bad Boy Records, 1997).

Public Enemy, "Fight the Power" in *Fear of a Black Planet* (CD; Def Jam Records, Columbia Records, 1990).

Queen Latifah, "Ladies First" in *All Hail the Queen* (CD; Tommy Boys Records, 1989).

Rick Ross, "Gunplay" in *Deeper Than Rap* (CD; Slip-n-Slide, Def Jam, 2009).

Rocko, "U.O.E.N.O., in *Gift of Gab 2* (CD; A1 Records, 2013).

Tech N9ne, "Like I Died" in *The Lost Scripts of K.O.D.* (CD; Strange Music, 2010).

Too Much Trouble, "Take the Pussy" in *Bringing Hell on Earth* (CD; Rap-A-Lot Records, 1992).

Trick Daddy, "Amerika," in *Thugs Are Us* featuring artist, Society (CD; Slip-n-Slide Records, 2001).

Tupac Shakur, "Keep Ya Head Up" in *Strictly 4 My Niggaz* (CD; Interscope Records, 1993).

Tyga, "Ice Cream Paintjob" in *King Shit* (CD; Mixtape, 2009).

Tyler The Creator, "Blow" in *Bastard* (CD; Self-released, 2009).

Young Jeezy, "My President," in *The Recession* (CD; Def Jam, 2008).

Young Money Entertainment, "Every Girl in the World" in *We Are Young Money* (CD; Young Money, Cash Money, Universal Motown, 2007).

Vado, "We Outchea" in *UNLostFiles* (CD; Self-released, 2012).

VIDEOGRAPHY

Boyz n the Hood. Directed by John Singleton. Columbia Pictures Corporation, 1991.

Malcolm X. Directed by Spike Lee. Warner Brothers Pictures, 1992.

Menace II Society. Directed by Albert and Allen Hughes. New Line Cinema, 1993.

Thug Life in D.C. Directed by Marc Levin. American Undercover. HBO, 1998.

INDEX

Page numbers in italics refer to tables and charts.

CPSIA information can be obtained at www.ICGtesting.com
Printed in the USA
LVOW05*2104311014

411470LV00008B/146/P